Modern Software Engineering

Modern Software Engineering

Ryan McNeil

CLANRYE
INTERNATIONAL
www.clanryeinternational.com

Clanrye International,
750 Third Avenue, 9ᵗʰ Floor,
New York, NY 10017, USA

ISBN: 978-1-64726-104-7

Cataloging-in-Publication Data

Modern software engineering / Ryan McNeil.
 p. cm.
Includes bibliographical references and index.
ISBN: 978-1-64726-104-7
1. Software engineering. 2. Computer programming. 3. Computer networks.
4. Computer science. 5. Information science. 6. Automatic programming
(Computer science). I. McNeil, Ryan.
QA76.758 .S64 2022
005.1--dc23

For information on all Clanrye International publications
visit our website at www.clanryeinternational.com

TABLE OF CONTENTS

Permissions

Index

It is with great pleasure that I present this book. It has been carefully written after numerous discussions with my peers and other practitioners of the field. I would like to take this opportunity to thank my family and friends who have been extremely supporting at every step in my life.

The collection of instructions which tell a computer how to work is known as software. The branch of computer science which deals with the application of engineering to develop software in a systematic method is referred to as software engineering. It involves the designing and implementation of complex computer programs. It is also concerned with the maintenance of such computer programs. Software engineering is an umbrella field that has various sub-disciplines. The most common of them include software design, software development and software testing. This book attempts to understand the multiple branches that fall under the discipline of software engineering and how such concepts have practical applications. Most of the topics introduced in this book cover new techniques and the applications of this field. It will provide comprehensive knowledge to the readers.

The chapters below are organized to facilitate a comprehensive understanding of the subject:

Chapter – Introduction to Software Engineering

The set of programs which is designed to perform a pre-defined function is known as computer software. There are various types of computer software such as system software, application software and programming software. This is an introductory chapter which will provide a brief introduction to software engineering and the different types of computer software.

Chapter – Fundamental Concepts in Software Engineering

There are a number of concepts which are considered to be fundamental to software engineering. A few of them are data modeling, continuous integration, software architecture and coupling. The chapter closely examines these key concepts of software engineering to provide an extensive understanding of the subject.

Chapter – Software Development

The process of designing, conceiving, programming, specifying, documenting and testing applications is known as software development. Its purpose is to create and maintain different software components. All the diverse aspects of software development have been carefully analyzed in this chapter.

Chapter – Software Testing

The investigation which is conducted in order to provide stakeholders with information regarding the quality of the software product is known as software testing. Some of the methods of testing software are functional testing, non-functional testing and operational acceptance testing. The topics elaborated in this chapter will help in gaining a better perspective about these methods of software testing.

Chapter – Applications of Software Engineering

Software engineering finds application in a variety of different fields. A few of these are systems development, computer aided design, computer graphics and web engineering. The diverse applications of software engineering in these fields have been thoroughly discussed in this chapter.

Ryan McNeil

Introduction to Software Engineering

The set of programs which is designed to perform a pre-defined function is known as computer software. There are various types of computer software such as system software, application software and programming software. This is an introductory chapter which will provide a brief introduction to software engineering and the different types of computer software.

COMPUTER SOFTWARE

Computer software is a program that enables a computer to perform a specific task, as opposed to the physical components of the system *(hardware)*. This includes application software such as a word processor, which enables a user to perform a task, and system software such as an operating system, which enables other software to run properly, by interfacing with hardware and with other software.

Starting in the 1980s, application software has been sold in mass-produced packages through retailers.

The term "software" was first used in this sense by John W. Tukey in 1957. In computer science and software engineering, computer software is all computer programs. The concept of reading different sequences of instructions into the memory of a device to control computations was invented by Charles Babbage as part of his difference engine.

Relationship to Hardware

Computer software is so called in contrast to computer hardware, which encompasses the physical interconnections and devices required to store and execute (or run) the software. In computers, software is loaded into random access memory (RAM) and executed in the central processing unit. At the lowest level, software consists of a machine language specific to an individual processor. The machine language consists of groups of binary values signifying processor instructions (object code), which change the state of the computer from its preceding state.

Software is an ordered sequence of instructions for changing the state of the computer hardware in a particular sequence. It is usually written in high-level programming languages that are easier and more efficient for humans to use (closer to natural language) than machine language. High-level languages are compiled or interpreted into machine language object code. Software may also be written in an assembly language, essentially, a mnemonic representation of a machine language using a natural language alphabet. Assembly language must be assembled into object code via an assembler.

Relationship to Data

Software has historically been considered an intermediary between electronic hardware and *data,* which are defined by the instructions defined by the *software.* As computational math becomes increasingly complex, the distinction between software and data becomes less precise. Data has generally been considered as either the output or input of executed software. However, data is not the only possible output or input. For example, (system) configuration information may also be considered input, although not *necessarily* considered data (and certainly not applications data). The output of a particular piece of executed software may be the input for another executed piece of software. Therefore, software may be considered an interface between hardware, data, and/or (other) software.

Computer Viruses

Computer viruses are a malignant type of computer program even though they might not be considered software. They can be created as any of the three types of software. Some viruses cause minor problems, such as slowing down a computer or using email to spread. Other viruses can cause more serious problems, such as destroying data or damaging hardware.

Program and Library

A program may not be sufficiently complete for execution by a computer. In particular, it may require additional software from a software library to be complete. Such a library may include software components used by stand-alone programs, but which cannot be executed on their own. Thus, programs may include standard routines that are common to many programs, extracted from these libraries. Libraries may also *include* stand-alone programs that are activated by some computer event and/or perform some function (such as computer "housekeeping") but do not return data to their activating program. Programs may be called by other programs and/or may call other programs.

Three Layers

Users often see things differently than programmers. People who use modern general purpose computers (as opposed to embedded systems, analog computers, supercomputers, and so forth) usually see three layers of software performing a variety of tasks: Platform, application, and user software.

- Platform software: Platform includes the basic input-output system (often described as *firmware* rather than *software*), device drivers, an operating system, and typically a graphical user interface which, in total, allow a user to interact with the computer and its peripherals (associated equipment). Platform software often comes bundled with the computer, and users may not realize that it exists or that they have a choice to use different platform software.

- Application software: Application software or simply, "Applications" are what most people think of when they think of software. Typical examples include office suites and video games. Application software is often purchased separately from computer hardware. Sometimes applications are bundled with the computer, but that does not change the fact that they run as independent applications. Applications are almost always independent programs from the operating system, though they are often tailored for specific platforms. Most users think of compilers, databases, and other "system software" as applications.

- User-written software: User software tailors systems to meet the users specific needs. User software includes spreadsheet templates, word processor macros, scientific simulations, and graphics and animation scripts. Even email filters are a kind of user software. Users create this software themselves and often overlook how important it is. Depending on how competently the user-written software has been integrated into purchased application packages, many users may not be aware of the distinction between the purchased packages, and what has been added by fellow co-workers.

Operation

Computer software has to be "loaded" into the computer's storage (also known as memory and RAM). Once the software is loaded, the computer is able to execute the software. Computers operate by *executing* the computer program. This involves passing instructions from the application software, through the system software, to the hardware which ultimately receives the instruction as machine code. Each instruction causes the computer to carry out an operation—moving data, carrying out a computation, or altering the control flow of instructions.

Data movement is typically from one place in memory to another. Sometimes it involves moving data between memory and registers which enable high-speed data access in the CPU.

A simple example of the way software operates is what happens when a user selects an entry such as "Copy" from a menu. In this case, a conditional instruction is executed to copy text from data in a "document" area residing in memory, perhaps to an intermediate storage area known as a "clipboard" data area. If a different menu entry such as "Paste" is chosen, the software may execute the instructions to copy the text from the clipboard data area to a specific location in the same or another document in memory.

Currently, almost the only limitations on the use of computer software in applications are the ingenuity of the designer/programmer. Consequently, large areas of activities (such as playing grand master level chess) formerly assumed to be impossible if done by software simulation is now routinely programmed. The only area that has so far proved reasonably secure from software simulation is the realm of human art—especially, pleasing music and literature.

Quality and Reliability

Software reliability considers the errors, faults, and failures related to the creation and operation of software. A lot of the quality and reliability of a program has to do with the Application software being written for specific System software. One example is that an application for an older System software may not work on a newer one.

Software Architecture

The software architecture of a system comprises its software components, their external properties, and their relationships with one another. The term also refers to documentation of a system's software architecture.

Describing Architectures

Architecture Description Languages

Architecture Description Languages (ADLs) are used to describe a Software Architecture. Several different ADLs have been developed by different organizations, including Wright (developed by Carnegie Mellon), Acme (developed by Carnegie Mellon), xADL (developed by UCI), Darwin (developed by Imperial College London), and DAOP-ADL (developed by University of Málaga). Common elements of an ADL are component, connector and configuration.

Views

Software architecture is commonly organized in views, which are analogous to the different types of blueprints made in building architecture.

Proprietary Software

Proprietary software is software that has restrictions on using and copying it, usually enforced by a proprietor. The prevention of use, copying, or modification can be achieved by legal or technical means. Technical means include releasing machine-readable binaries only, and withholding the human-readable source code. Legal means can involve software licensing, copyright, and patent law. Proprietary software can be sold for money as commercial software or available at zero-price as freeware. The monopoly provided by proprietary software allows a distributor of commercial copies to charge any price for those copies. Distributors of proprietary software have more control over what users can do with the software than nonproprietary software.

Free Software

Free software, as defined by the Free Software Foundation, is software which can be used, copied, studied, modified, and redistributed without restriction. Freedom from such restrictions is central to the concept, with the opposite of free software being proprietary software (a distinction unrelated to whether a fee is charged). The usual way for software to be distributed as free software is for the software to be licensed to the recipient with a free software license (or be in the public domain), and the source code of the software to be made available (for a compiled language). Most free software is distributed online without charge, or off-line at the marginal cost of distribution, but this is not required, and people may sell copies for any price.

To help distinguish *libre* (freedom) software from *gratis* (zero price) software, Richard Stallman, founder of the free software movement, developed the following explanation: "Free software is a matter of liberty, not price. To understand the concept, you should think of 'free' as in 'free speech', not as in 'free beer.'" More specifically, free software means that computer users have the freedom to cooperate with whom they choose, and to control the software they use.

Open-source Software

Open-source software is computer software whose source code is available under a copyright license that permits users to study, change, and improve the software, and to redistribute it in modified or unmodified form. It is the most prominent example of open source development.

In 1998, a group of individuals advocated that the term "free software" be replaced by open-source software (OSS) as an expression which is less ambiguous and more comfortable for the corporate world. Software developers may want to publish their software with an open-source software license, so that anybody may also develop the same software or understand how it works. Open-source software generally allows anybody to make a new version of the software, port it to new operating systems and processor architectures, share it with others or market it. The aim of open source is to let the product be more understandable, modifiable, duplicable, reliable, or simply accessible, while it is still marketable.

The Open Source Definition, notably, presents an open-source philosophy, and further defines a boundary on the usage, modification and redistribution of open-source software. Software licenses grant rights to users which would otherwise be prohibited by copyright. These include rights on usage, modification and redistribution. Several open-source software licenses have qualified within the boundary of the Open Source Definition. The most prominent example is the popular GNU General Public License (GPL). While open source presents a way to broadly make the sources of a product publicly accessible, the open-source licenses allow the authors to fine tune such access.

Freeware

Freeware is copyrighted computer software which is made available for use free of charge, for an unlimited time, as opposed to shareware, in which the user is required to pay (for example, after some trial period). The only criterion for being classified as "freeware" is that the software must be made available for use for an unlimited time at no cost. The software license may impose one or more other restrictions on the type of use including personal use, individual use, non-profit use, non-commercial use, academic use, commercial use or any combination of these. For instance, the license may be "free for personal, non-commercial use." There is some software that may be considered freeware, but that have limited distribution; that is, they may only be downloaded from a specific site, and they can not be redistributed. Hence, such software wouldn't be freely redistributable software. According to the basic definition, that software would be freeware; according to stricter definitions, they wouldn't be. Everything created with the freeware programs can be distributed at no cost (for example graphic, documents, waves made by user).

Freeware contrasts with free software, because of the different meanings of the word "free." Freeware is gratis and refers to zero price, versus free software that is described as "libre," which means free to study, change, copy, redistribute, share, and use the software in any purpose. However, many programs are both freeware and free software. They are available for zero price, provide the source code and are distributed with free software permissions. This software would exclusively be called free software to avoid confusion with freeware that usually does not come with the source code and is therefore proprietary software.

Shareware

Shareware is a marketing method for commercial software, whereby a trial version is distributed in advance and without payment, as is common for proprietary software. Shareware software is typically obtained free of charge, either by downloading from the Internet or on magazine cover-disks. A user tries out the program, and thus shareware has also been known as "try before you buy," demoware, trialware, and by many other names. A shareware program is accompanied by a request for payment, and the software's distribution license often requires such a payment. Payment is often required once a set period of time has elapsed after installation.

Types of Computer Software

System Software

System software coordinates the activities and functions of hardware and software, and it controls the operations of computer hardware and provides an environment or platform for all the other types of software to work in. It is the most basic type of software in any computer system, which is essential for other programs, applications and the whole computer system to function. (System software examples – Microsoft Windows XP, Mac OS, Linux, Windows Vista, Ubuntu, device drivers, etc.)

Application Software

Application software is what helps the user perform the tasks of his/her choice. They are non-essential software which are installed and run, depending upon the requirements, in the environment provided by the system software. (Application software examples – MS Office, Open Office, Media Players, MS Access, educational software, media development software, Antivirus software, etc.)

Programming Software

Programming software is used to write, test, debug and develop other software programs and applications. The various programming language editors such as Eclipse – a Java language editor – appear under this category. They are used for creating both the system as well as application software. (Programming software examples – Turbo C, Xilinx, Kiel, compilers, debuggers, Integrated Development Environment (IDE), etc.)

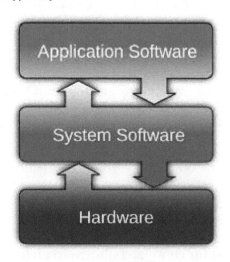

Sub-types of Computer Software

Apart from the above main types of software there are many other subtypes, which will be mentioned below:

- Freeware – Freeware is a type of software that anyone can download from the Internet and use for free. (Examples – Google Talk, Yahoo Messenger, uTorrent, etc.)

- Shareware – Shareware is usually distributed for free on a trial basis. It can be shared without violation of any laws. They usually stop working or prompt the user to purchase the full version, once the trial period expires. (Examples – BearShare, Kazaa, Winzip, etc.)

- Registry Cleaners – When you install a lot of software – or games for example – your computer's registry becomes clogged. Registry cleaners are used to clean up or delete all the invalid registry entries which has the benefit of speeding up your computer. (Examples- TuneUp Utilities, Eusing, etc.)

- Content Control Software – This kind of software allows you to control the content that can be accessed by a user on a computer. They are mostly used for restricting access over the Internet. (Example- K9 Web Protection, PGSurfer, etc.)

- Project Management Software – As its name suggests, project management software is a software package that helps multiple users to work on a project simultaneously. It allows them to schedule events, network with the other users, allocate resources, etc. (Example- Microsoft Office Project Server, HyperOffice, 24SevenOffice, etc.)

- Utility Software – These are usually small programs that help the management of the hardware and the application software installed on a computer. (Example- Disk defragmenters, Disk cleaners, etc.)

- Open Source Software – This is a type of software for which the source code is available to all users (open). As such, anyone can make changes to it and release their own new version. (Example – Linux, Android OS, OpenOffice, etc.)

- Web Browsers – Browsers are programs that allow you to surf or browse web pages on the Internet. (Example – Internet Explorer, Safari, Mozilla Firefox, etc.)

With constant advancements in the field of software engineering, several new software and applications are being developed every day. Hence, the list provided above shouldn't be considered definitive, as in the coming years, many more newer types of software would have been developed.

SOFTWARE TOOLS AND TECHNIQUES

Software Tools, Software Techniques, Benefits, Classification of Software Tools and Techniques, Glossaries of Software Tools and Techniques. The complexities of writing and maintaining programs have caused software costs to outstrip computer hardware costs. Recent studies predict that by 1990, more than 90 percent of the cost of data processing will be attributable to software.

During the 1970s, private industry and government spent more than $8 billion a year on software. Experts believe that such expenditures currently exceed $20 billion yearly. Because of such sky-rocketing costs, software tools and techniques are emerging that facilitate the development effort through streamlined procedures or automation of some development tasks.

Many tools and techniques have been developed that offer significantly improved management control and reduced costs if properly applied. The number of new tools and techniques continues to grow.

This topic discusses the use of software tools and techniques to alleviate the problems of development, maintenance, modification, operation, and conversion of applications software. Many of the software tools and techniques discussed are available for all types of computers. Software tools and techniques can be valuable aids to information resource managers; data processing design, development, and operations staff; and EDP auditors. In addition, this article provides a glossary of the most common types of software tools and techniques and a method for productively classifying and managing them.

Software Tools

A software tool is a program that automates some of the labor involved in the management, design, coding, testing, inspection, or maintenance of other programs. Commercially available tools range in size and complexity from simple aids for individual programmers and end users to complex tools that can support many software projects simultaneously. The following are some common tools:

- Preprocessors: Preprocessors perform preliminary work on a draft computer program before it is completely tested on the computer. Types of preprocessors include filters (also known as code auditors), which allow management to determine quickly whether programmers are adhering to specifications and standards, and shorthand preprocessors, which allow programmers and end users to write the programs in an abbreviated form that is then expanded by the preprocessor before it is tested on the computer. Shorthand pre processors reduce writing, keypunching, and proofreading effort.

- Program analyzers: These tools modify or monitor the operation of an applications program to allow information about its operating characteristics to be collected automatically. This information can then be used to help modify the program to reduce its run cost or to verify that the program operates correctly.

- Online programming support programs: These tools enable programmers and users to quickly correct and modify applications programs and test program results.

- Test data generators: These tools analyze a program and produce files of data needed to test the logic of the program.

Software Techniques

Software techniques are methods or procedures for designing, developing, 'documenting, and maintaining programs, or for managing these activities. There are generally two types of software techniques: those used by personnel who work on programs and those used by managers to control the work.

Examples of software techniques useful to workers include:

- Structured programming: Developing programs in a certain style with standard constructs so that they will be more easily understood by others who must later maintain and modify them, which facilitates documentation, testing, and correction:

    ○ Operating Environment

    ○ Mainframes

    ○ Minicomputers

    ○ Microcomouters

- Top-down development: Designing, coding, and testing systems by building program modules starting with those at the general level and proceeding down to the most specialized, detailed level.

- Performance improvement: Analysis and modification of programs to make them run more efficiently without affecting user requirements. Performance may be improved by various software tools, including program analyzers.

- Concurrent documentation: The development of documentation concurrently with program development to provide better project control, increase completeness of the documentation, and save money.

Examples of techniques useful to managers include:

- Third-party inspection of software to improve quality: It is now feasible to require such inspection because current tools can automate much of the work involved.

- Chief programmer team method: The team nucleus is a skilled chief programmer, a backup programmer, and a programming librarian.

- Alternatives to software development: This applies to both software tools and applications software.

Benefits of Software Tools and Techniques

Software tools and techniques can be powerful aids in the design, development, testing, and maintenance of software. Several studies have reported that the application of tools and techniques result in significant benefits, including improved management control, equipment procurements that could be deferred and reduced software costs specifically the use of software tools and techniques can:

- Reduce adverse impact on user tasks: Structured programming produces programs that are easier to test and, once tested, easier to modify. Therefore, structured programming can reduce the chances of errors in the user results (e.g., overpayments) and make it easier to respond quickly to future user requests for modifications. In addition, appropriate tools can reduce the work of verifying that test data has actually exercised a program. This improves the chances of removing errors from the program before it is placed into production.

- Reduce overruns and delays: Current design and development techniques, including structured programming, can make software development more visible to management and more controllable.

- Reduce redundant software projects-software tools and techniques make it easier for organizations to reuse existing software and avoid the expense and delay of developing their own software. Tools reduce the labor of analyzing software for suitability; modern techniques give a better idea of what to analyze for.

- Reduce software conversion costs: As noted in various studies and expounded by conversion contractors, appropriate tools can significantly reduce the labor of making programs written for one type of computer run on another.

- Allow equipment purchases to be deferred: Newly written software requires fewer machine resources to run, and existing software can be modified to reduce required machine resource utilization.

- Reduce operating costs: This includes the labor costs of maintenance, modification, and conversion, as well as the cost of the machine resources required to run the software.

- Improve software quality: Improved quality reduces testing and revision and simplifies future maintenance, modification, and conversion.

An organization that adopts a carefully selected group of software tools and techniques can better predict software costs and provide better documentation. For example, some organizations have adopted and required the use of a group of modern programming tools and techniques, including structured programming, a program support library, structured design, concurrent documentation, and preprocessors. The reported benefits include improved project control, better end products, better organization for the maintenance phase, and estimated annual savings of more than $1 million in the development and maintenance of systems.

Software quality can be improved by applying appropriate tools and techniques in the development phase. Software tools can reduce the labor of preparing test data and verifying that the test data has exercised all program logic. More thorough testing becomes feasible and more reliable programs result.

One management technique to improve the quality of software systems requires the use of quality control groups independent of the software developers. This quality control can be performed by performance evaluation groups or internal auditors. These groups can review either software development or maintenance projects. For example, two recent government reports highlight cases in which internal auditors' use of software tools and techniques resulted in the detection and correction of errors before system implementation and eliminated unnecessary program instructions.

Classification of Software Tools and Techniques

Software tools and techniques assist the analyst, manager, programmer, and user by providing meaningful information and can be used to automate parts of the software effort, thereby increasing software reliability and productivity. Most important, they can be reused for multiple projects with diverse needs, distributing their development costs and thus lowering the cost to individual projects.

A life cycle concept for developing a method of classifying software tools and techniques. The basic model of the software life cycle process has been developed in accordance with the standard definitions of a software life cycle. This model illustrates the managerial, methodological, and evaluative techniques required throughout the cycle. The managerial techniques necessary over a software life cycle involve:

- Managing people: The users, systems analyst, programmers, project manager, test personnel.

- Managing a project: Planning, coordination, direction, control, review.

- Managing the configuration: Change control, documentation control, modification control, upgrade, optimization.

- Using quality assurance as a verifying agent.

The methodological techniques involve:

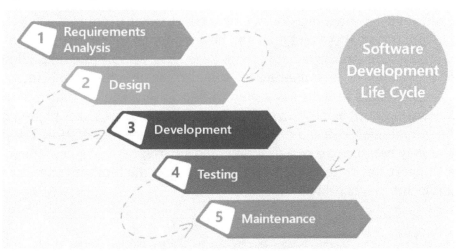

Software Life Cycle Taxonomy.

- Integrating current and new technology (e.g., structured design concepts, programming, programmer's workbench, utilities, new software tools) into the design, development, and operational stages of the software life.

- Using methods to improve the productivity of the designers, developers, testers, quality assurance personnel, and auditors.

- Using methods for transferring the knowledge gained to other projects and people (e.g., training, seminars, professional papers, conferences, software decomposition and migration, tool migration).

The evaluative techniques required involve the better use of metrics and cost data to assess the implications of and risk caused by environmental changes. Examples of such metrics are resource estimators, factor analyzers, reliability models, and product measures. The basis for software life cycle evaluation is cost; therefore, accurate cost accounting for DP resources, especially in software, is a critical element.

The National Bureau of Standards (NBS) has developed taxonomy for classifying general-purpose software tools in the DP environment. The taxonomy was published as Federal Information Processing Standard (FIPS) 99, "Guideline: A Framework for the Evaluation and Comparison of Software Development Tools." Because such a wide range of tool packages could be encompassed by the term general purpose, that term was applied only to those software tool packages usually not provided by the vendor as part of the purchased system.

The goals established for the taxonomy were to:

- Permit existing tools to be uniquely classified;

- Allow tool needs to be easily specified;

- Provide a simple and meaningful set of descriptors for each tool classification;

- Permit tool capabilities, costs, and benefits to be compared within a given classification.

The characterization of software tools represents a major challenge because most tool descriptions fail to provide sufficient information. Considerable effort may be required to glean the information necessary to identify what the tool does and how it interfaces with the external environment. Once identified, these facts are extremely useful. Specifying what a tool does allows meaningful comparison of the capabilities of competing tools. It also permits the establishment of criteria for selecting tools (i.e., costs and benefits associated with tool usage can be related to tool capabilities and evaluated accordingly). Specification of a tool's interface enables a user to determine if the tool can produce the output needed and if it can work within the given operational environment. For example, the tool may become part of a programming environment (e.g., an integrated collection of tools used to support software development). In this case, the tool's interfaces with other tools are an important factor in tool evaluation.

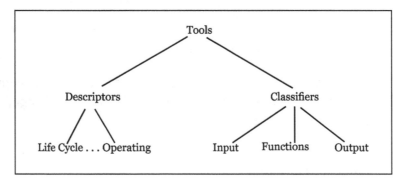

Tool Description and Classification Interrelationships.

This Federal Information Processing Standard is explicit in the specifications of features in all three dimensions (i.e., input, functions, output), achieving a primary objective-a unique classification of an individual tool or a tool need. Products are classified according to a features designator called the taxonomy key. The key is formed by combining the individual feature keys for each of the three dimensions of the taxonomy. As many individual designators are chosen in each dimension as are necessary to completely describe the tool. The key, as illustrated in figure, clearly and succinctly communicates the results of classification in all three dimensions.

SOFTWARE ENGINEERING

Software engineering is the application of principles used in the field of engineering, which usually deals with physical systems, to the design, development, testing, deployment and management of software systems. The field of software engineering applies the disciplined, structured approach to programming that is used in engineering to software development with the stated goal of improving the quality, time and budget efficiency, along with the assurance of structured testing and engineer certification.

Software engineering is typically used for large and intricate software systems rather than single applications or programs. Development, however, is simply one phase of the process. While a software engineer is typically responsible for the design of systems, programmers are often responsible for coding its implementation.

Software engineering involves a number of fields that cover the process of engineering software and certification including: requirements gathering, software design, software construction, software maintenance, software configuration management, software engineering managent, software development process management and creation, software engineering models and methods, software quality, software engineering professional practices as well as foundational computing and mathematical and engineering study.

Though the original use of the term is uncertain, the first software engineering conference was held and sponsored by NATO in 1968. The conference addressed the inconsistency and unreliability in software development as well as the need for better quality and reliability. The conference gathered international experts who agreed the systematic approach of physical world engineering should be applied to software development, as it already was developed with those goals in mind.

Fundamental Concepts in Software Engineering

There are a number of concepts which are considered to be fundamental to software engineering. A few of them are data modeling, continuous integration, software architecture and coupling. The chapter closely examines these key concepts of software engineering to provide an extensive understanding of the subject.

SOFTWARE QUALITY ASSURANCE

Software quality assurance (SQA) is a process which assures that all software engineering processes, methods, activities and work items are monitored and comply against the defined standards. These defined standards could be one or a combination of any like ISO 9000, CMMI model, ISO15504, etc. SQA incorporates all software development processes starting from defining requirements to coding until release. Its prime goal is to ensure quality.

Software Quality Assurance Plan

Abbreviated as SQAP, the software quality assurance plan comprises of the procedures, techniques, and tools that are employed to make sure that a product or service aligns with the requirements defined in the SRS (software requirement specification).

The plan identifies the SQA responsibilities of a team, lists the areas that need to be reviewed and audited. It also identifies the SQA work products.

The SQA plan document consists of the below sections:

1. Purpose section,

2. Reference section,

3. Software configuration management section,

4. Problem reporting and corrective action section,

5. Tools, technologies and methodologies section,

6. Code control section,

7. Records: Collection, maintenance and retention section,

8. Testing methodology.

SQA Activities

1. Creating an SQA Management Plan: The foremost activity includes laying down a proper plan regarding how the SQA will be carried out in your project. Along with what SQA approach you are going to follow, what engineering activities will be carried out, and it also includes ensuring that you have a right talent mix in your team.

2. Setting the Checkpoints: The SQA team sets up different checkpoints according to which it evaluates the quality of the project activities at each checkpoint/project stage. This ensures regular quality inspection and working as per the schedule.

3. Apply software Engineering Techniques: Applying some software engineering techniques aids a software designer in achieving high-quality specification. For gathering information, a designer may use techniques such as interviews and FAST (Functional Analysis System Technique). Later, based on the information gathered, the software designer can prepare the project estimation using techniques like WBS (work breakdown structure), SLOC (source line of codes), and FP(functional point) estimation.

4. Executing Formal Technical Reviews: An FTR is done to evaluate the quality and design of the prototype. In this process, a meeting is conducted with the technical staff to discuss regarding the actual quality requirements of the software and the design quality of the prototype. This activity helps in detecting errors in the early phase of SDLC and reduces rework effort in the later phases.

5. Having a Multi- Testing Strategy: By multi-testing strategy, we mean that one should not rely on any single testing approach, instead, multiple types of testing should be performed so that the software product can be tested well from all angles to ensure better quality.

6. Enforcing Process Adherence: This activity insists the need for process adherence during the software development process. The development process should also stick to the defined procedures.

This activity is a blend of two sub-activities which are explained below in detail:

- Product Evaluation: This activity confirms that the software product is meeting the requirements that were discovered in the project management plan. It ensures that the set standards for the project are followed correctly.

- Process Monitoring: This activity verifies if the correct steps were taken during software development. This is done by matching the actually taken steps against the documented steps.

7. Controlling Change: In this activity, we use a mix of manual procedures and automated tools to have a mechanism for change control. By validating the change requests, evaluating the nature of change and controlling the change effect, it is ensured that the software quality is maintained during the development and maintenance phases.

8. Measure Change Impact: If any defect is reported by the QA team, then the concerned team fixes the defect. After this, the QA team should determine the impact of the change which is brought by this defect fix. They need to test not only if the change has fixed the defect, but also if the change is compatible with the whole project. For this purpose, we use software quality metrics which allows managers and developers to observe the activities and proposed changes from the beginning till the end of SDLC and initiate corrective action wherever required.

9. Performing SQA Audits: The SQA audit inspects the entire actual SDLC process followed by comparing it against the established process. It also checks whatever reported by the team in the status reports were actually performed or not. This activity also exposes any non-compliance issues.

10. Maintaining Records and Reports: It is crucial to keep the necessary documentation related to SQA and share the required SQA information with the stakeholders. The test results, audit results, review reports, change requests documentation, etc. should be kept for future reference.

11. Manage Good Relations: In fact, it is very important to maintain harmony between the QA and the development team.

We often hear that testers and developers often feel superior to each other. This should be avoided as it can affect the overall project quality.

Software Quality Assurance Standards

In general, SQA may demand conformance to one or more standards. Some of the most popular standards are discussed below:

ISO 9000: This standard is based on seven quality management principles which help the organizations to ensure that their products or services are aligned with the customer needs'.

7 principles of ISO 9000 are depicted in the below image:

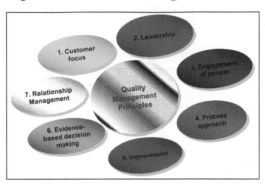

1. CMMI level: CMMI stands for Capability maturity model Integration. This model was originated in software engineering. It can be employed to direct process improvement throughout a project, department, or an entire organization.

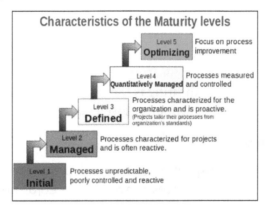

An organization is appraised and awarded a maturity level rating (1-5) based on the type of appraisal.

2. Test Maturity Model integration (TMMi): Based on CMMi, this model focuses on maturity levels in software quality management and testing.

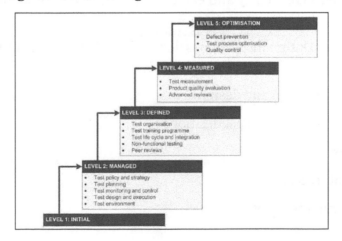

As an organization moves on a higher maturity level, it achieves a higher capability for producing high-quality products with fewer defects and closely meets the business requirements.

Elements of Software Quality Assurance

- Software engineering Standards
- Technical reviews and audits
- Software Testing for quality control
- Error collection and analysis
- Change management
- Educational programs
- Vendor management
- Security management
- Safety
- Risk management

SQA Techniques

There are several techniques for SQA. Auditing is the chief technique that is widely adopted. However, we have a few other significant techniques as well.

Various SQA Techniques include:

- Auditing: Auditing involves inspection of the work products and its related information to determine if the set of standard processes were followed or not.

- Reviewing: A meeting in which the software product is examined by both the internal and external stakeholders to seek their comments and approval.

- Code Inspection: It is the most formal kind of review that does static testing to find bugs and avoid defect growth in the later stages. It is done by a trained mediator/peer and is based on rules, checklist, entry and exit criteria. The reviewer should not be the author of the code.

- Design Inspection: Design inspection is done using a checklist that inspects the below areas of software design:
  - General requirements and design
  - Functional and Interface specifications
  - Conventions
  - Requirement traceability
  - Structures and interfaces
  - Logic
  - Performance

- ◦ Error handling and recovery

- ◦ Testability, extensibility

- ◦ Coupling and cohesion

- Simulation: Simulation is a tool that models the real-life situation in order to virtually examine the behavior of the system under study.

- Functional Testing: It is a QA technique which verifies what the system does without considering how it does. This type of black box testing mainly focuses on testing the system specifications or features.

- Standardization: Standardization plays a crucial role in quality assurance. It decreases the ambiguity and guesswork, thus ensuring quality.

- Static Analysis: It is a software analysis that is done by an automated tool without actually executing the program. This technique is highly used for quality assurance in medical, nuclear and aviation software. Software metrics and reverse engineering are some popular forms of static analysis.

- Walkthroughs: Software walkthrough or code walkthrough is a kind of peer review where the developer guides the members of the development team to go through the product and raise queries, suggest alternatives, make comments regarding possible errors, standard violations or any other issues.

- Path Testing: It is a white box testing technique where the complete branch coverage is ensured by executing each independent path at least once.

- Stress Testing: This type of testing is done to check how robust a system is by testing it under heavy load i.e. beyond normal conditions.

- Six Sigma: Six Sigma is a quality assurance approach that aims at nearly perfect products or services. It is widely applied in many fields including software. The main objective of six sigma is process improvement so that the produced software is 99.76 % defect free.

SOFTWARE MAINTENANCE

Software maintenance in software engineering is the modification of a software product after delivery to correct faults, to improve performance or other attributes.

A common perception of maintenance is that it merely involves fixing defects. However, one study indicated that over 80% of maintenance effort is used for non-corrective actions. This perception is perpetuated by users submitting problem reports that in reality are functionality enhancements to the system. More recent studies put the bug-fixing proportion closer to 21%.

Importance of Software Maintenance

The key software maintenance issues are both managerial and technical. Key management issues are: alignment with customer priorities, staffing, which organization does maintenance, estimating costs. Key technical issues are: limited understanding, impact analysis, testing, maintainability measurement. Software maintenance is a very broad activity that includes error correction, enhancements of capabilities, deletion of obsolete capabilities, and optimization. Because change is inevitable, mechanisms must be developed for evaluation, controlling and making modifications.

So any work done to change the software after it is in operation is considered to be maintenance work. The purpose is to preserve the value of software over the time. The value can be enhanced by expanding the customer base, meeting additional requirements, becoming easier to use, more efficient and employing newer technology. Maintenance may span for 20 years, whereas development may be 1–2 years.

Software Maintenance Planning

An integral part of software is the maintenance one, which requires an accurate maintenance plan to be prepared during the software development. It should specify how users will request modifications or report problems. The budget should include resource and cost estimates. A new decision should be addressed for the developing of every new system feature and its quality objectives. The software maintenance, which can last for 5–6 years (or even decades) after the development process, calls for an effective plan which can address the scope of software maintenance, the tailoring of the post delivery/deployment process, the designation of who will provide maintenance, and an estimate of the life-cycle costs. The selection of proper enforcement of standards is the challenging task right from early stage of software engineering which has not got definite importance by the concerned stakeholders.

Software Maintenance Processes

The six software maintenance processes are:

1. The implementation process contains software preparation and transition activities, such as the conception and creation of the maintenance plan; the preparation for handling problems identified during development; and the follow-up on product configuration management.

2. The problem and modification analysis process, which is executed once the application has become the responsibility of the maintenance group. The maintenance programmer must analyze each request, confirm it (by reproducing the situation) and check its validity, investigate it and propose a solution, document the request and the solution proposal, and finally, obtain all the required authorizations to apply the modifications.

3. The process considering the implementation of the modification itself.

4. The process acceptance of the modification, by confirming the modified work with the individual who submitted the request in order to make sure the modification provided a solution.

5. The migration process (platform migration, for example) is exceptional, and is not part of daily maintenance tasks. If the software must be ported to another platform without any change in functionality, this process will be used and a maintenance project team is likely to be assigned to this task.

6. Finally, the last maintenance process, also an event which does not occur on a daily basis, is the retirement of a piece of software.

There are a number of processes, activities and practices that are unique to maintainers, for example:

- Transition: A controlled and coordinated sequence of activities during which a system is transferred progressively from the developer to the maintainer;

- Service Level Agreements (SLAs) and specialized (domain-specific) maintenance contracts negotiated by maintainers;

- Modification Request and Problem Report Help Desk: A problem-handling process used by maintainers to prioritize, documents and route the requests they receive.

Categories of Maintenance in ISO/IEC 14764

E.B. Swanson initially identified three categories of maintenance: corrective, adaptive, and perfective. The IEEE 1219 standard was superseded in June 2010 by P14764. These have since been updated and ISO/IEC 14764 presents:

- Corrective maintenance: Reactive modification of a software product performed after delivery to correct discovered problems.

- Adaptive maintenance: Modification of a software product performed after delivery to keep a software product usable in a changed or changing environment.

- Perfective maintenance: Modification of a software product after delivery to improve performance or maintainability.

- Preventive maintenance: Modification of a software product after delivery to detect and correct latent faults in the software product before they become effective faults.

There is also a notion of pre-delivery/pre-release maintenance which is all the good things you do to lower the total cost of ownership of the software. Things like compliance with coding standards that includes software maintainability goals. The management of coupling and cohesion of the software. The attainment of software supportability goals (SAE JA1004, JA1005 and JA1006 for example). Note also that some academic institutions are carrying out research to quantify the cost to ongoing software maintenance due to the lack of resources such as design documents and system/software comprehension training and resources (multiply costs by approx. 1.5-2.0 where there is no design data available).

Maintenance Factors

Impact of key adjustment factors on maintenance (sorted in order of maximum positive impact):

Maintenance Factors	Plus Range
Maintenance specialists	35%
High staff experience	34%

Table-driven variables and data	33%
Low complexity of base code	32%
Y2K and special search engines	30%
Code restructuring tools	29%
Re-engineering tools	27%
High level programming languages	25%
Reverse engineering tools	23%
Complexity analysis tools	20%
Defect tracking tools	20%
Y2K "mass update" specialists	20%
Automated change control tools	18%
Unpaid overtime	18%
Quality measurements	16%
Formal base code inspections	15%
Regression test libraries	15%
Excellent response time	12%
Annual training of > 10 days	12%
High management experience	12%
HELP desk automation	12%
No error prone modules	10%
On-line defect reporting	10%
Productivity measurements	8%
Excellent ease of use	7%
User satisfaction measurements	5%
High team morale	5%
Sum	503%

Not only are error-prone modules troublesome, but many other factors can degrade performance too. For example, very complex spaghetti code is quite difficult to maintain safely. A very common situation which often degrades performance is lack of suitable maintenance tools, such as defect tracking software, change management software, and test library software. Below describe some of the factors and the range of impact on software maintenance.

Impact of key adjustment factors on maintenance (sorted in order of maximum negative impact):

Maintenance Factors	Minus Range
Error prone modules	-50%
Embedded variables and data	-45%
Staff inexperience	-40%
High code complexity	-30%
No Y2K of special search engines	-28%
Manual change control methods	-27%
Low level programming languages	-25%
No defect tracking tools	-24%

No Y2K "mass update" specialists	-22%
Poor ease of use	-18%
No quality measurements	-18%
No maintenance specialists	-18%
Poor response time	-16%
No code inspections	-15%
No regression test libraries	-15%
No help desk automation	-15%
No on-line defect reporting	-12%
Management inexperience	-15%
No code restructuring tools	-10%
No annual training	-10%
No reengineering tools	-10%
No reverse-engineering tools	-10%
No complexity analysis tools	-10%
No productivity measurements	-7%
Poor team morale	-6%
No user satisfaction measurements	-4%
No unpaid overtime	0%
Sum	-500%

Types of Software Maintenance

There are four types of maintenance, namely, corrective, adaptive, perfective, and preventive. Corrective maintenance is concerned with fixing errors that are observed when the software is in use. Adaptive maintenance is concerned with the change in the software that takes place to make the software adaptable to new environment such as to run the software on a new operating system. Perfective maintenance is concerned with the change in the software that occurs while adding new functionalities in the software. Preventive maintenance involves implementing changes to prevent the occurrence of errors. The distribution of types of maintenance by type and by percentage of time consumed.

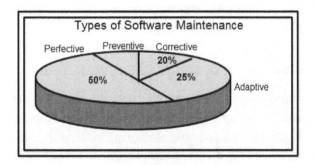

Corrective maintenance deals with the repair of faults or defects found in day-today system functions. A defect can result due to errors in software design, logic and coding. Design errors occur when changes made to the software are incorrect, incomplete, wrongly communicated, or the change request is misunderstood. Logical errors result from invalid tests and conclusions, incorrect implementation of design specifications, faulty logic flow, or incomplete test of data. All these errors, referred to as residual errors, prevent the software from conforming to its agreed specifications. Note that the need for corrective maintenance is usually initiated by bug reports drawn by the users.

In the event of a system failure due to an error, actions are taken to restore the operation of the software system. The approach in corrective maintenance is to locate the original specifications in order to determine what the system was originally designed to do. However, due to pressure from management, the maintenance team sometimes resorts to emergency fixes known as patching. Corrective maintenance accounts for 20% of all the maintenance activities.

Adaptive Maintenance

Adaptive maintenance is the implementation of changes in a part of the system, which has been affected by a change that occurred in some other part of the system. Adaptive maintenance consists of adapting software to changes in the environment such as the hardware or the operating system. The term environment in this context refers to the conditions and the influences which act (from outside) on the system. For example, business rules, work patterns, and government policies have a significant impact on the software system.

For instance, a government policy to use a single 'European currency' will have a significant effect on the software system. An acceptance of this change will require banks in various member countries to make significant changes in their software systems to accommodate this currency. Adaptive maintenance accounts for 25% of all the maintenance activities.

Perfective Maintenance

Perfective maintenance mainly deals with implementing new or changed user requirements. Perfective maintenance involves making functional enhancements to the system in addition to the activities to increase the system's performance even when the changes have not been suggested by faults. This includes enhancing both the function and efficiency of the code and changing the functionalities of the system as per the users' changing needs.

Examples of perfective maintenance include modifying the payroll program to incorporate a new union settlement and adding a new report in the sales analysis system. Perfective maintenance accounts for 50%, that is, the largest of all the maintenance activities.

Preventive Maintenance

Preventive maintenance involves performing activities to prevent the occurrence of errors. It tends to reduce the software complexity thereby improving program understandability and increasing software maintainability. It comprises documentation updating, code optimization, and code restructuring. Documentation updating involves modifying the documents affected by the changes in order to correspond to the present state of the system. Code optimization involves modifying the programs for faster execution or efficient use of storage space. Code restructuring involves transforming the program structure for reducing the complexity in source code and making it easier to understand.

Preventive maintenance is limited to the maintenance organization only and no external requests are acquired for this type of maintenance. Preventive maintenance accounts for only 5% of all the maintenance activities.

DATA MODELING

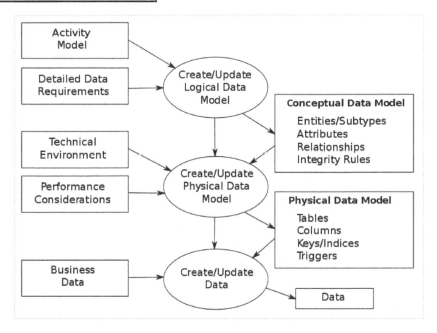

The data modeling process: The figure illustrates the way data models are developed and used today.

A conceptual data model is developed based on the data requirements for the application that is being developed, perhaps in the context of an activity model. The data model will normally consist of entity types, attributes, relationships, integrity rules, and the definitions of those objects. This is then used as the start point for interface or database design

Data modeling in software engineering is the process of creating a data model for an information system by applying certain formal techniques. Data modeling is a process used to define and analyze data requirements needed to support the business processes within the scope of corresponding information systems in organizations. Therefore, the process of data modeling involves professional data modelers working closely with business stakeholders, as well as potential users of the information system.

There are three different types of data models produced while progressing from requirements to the actual database to be used for the information system. The data requirements are initially recorded as a conceptual data model which is essentially a set of technology independent specifications about the data and is used to discuss initial requirements with the business stakeholders. The conceptual model is then translated into a logical data model, which documents structures of the data that can be implemented in databases. Implementation of one conceptual data model may require multiple logical data models. The last step in data modeling is transforming the logical data model to a physical data model that organizes the data into tables, and accounts for access, performance and storage details. Data modeling defines not just data elements, but also their structures and the relationships between them.

Data modeling techniques and methodologies are used to model data in a standard, consistent, predictable manner in order to manage it as a resource. The use of data modeling standards is strongly recommended for all projects requiring a standard means of defining and analyzing data within an organization, e.g., using data modeling:

- To assist business analysts, programmers, testers, manual writers, IT package selectors, engineers, managers, related organizations and clients to understand and use an agreed semi-formal model the concepts of the organization and how they relate to one another.

- To manage data as a resource.

- For the integration of information systems.

- For designing databases/data warehouses (aka data repositories).

Data modeling may be performed during various types of projects and in multiple phases of projects. Data models are progressive; there is no such thing as the final data model for a business or application. Instead a data model should be considered a living document that will change in response to a changing business. The data models should ideally be stored in a repository so that they can be retrieved, expanded, and edited over time. Whitten et al. determined two types of data modeling:

- Strategic data modeling: This is part of the creation of an information systems strategy, which defines an overall vision and architecture for information systems. Information technology engineering is a methodology that embraces this approach.

- Data modeling during systems analysis: In systems analysis logical data models are created as part of the development of new databases.

Data modeling is also used as a technique for detailing business requirements for specific databases. It is sometimes called *database modeling* because a data model is eventually implemented in a database.

Data models

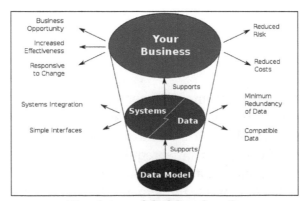

How data models deliver benefit.

Data models provide a framework for data to be used within information systems by providing specific definition and format. If a data model is used consistently across systems then compatibility of data can be achieved. If the same data structures are used to store and access data then different applications can share data seamlessly. The results of this are indicated in the diagram. However, systems and interfaces are often expensive to build, operate, and maintain. They may also constrain the business rather than support it. This may occur when the quality of the data models implemented in systems and interfaces is poor.

Some common problems found in data models are:

- Business rules, specific to how things are done in a particular place, are often fixed in the structure of a data model. This means that small changes in the way business is conducted lead to large changes in computer systems and interfaces. So, business rules need to be implemented in a flexible way that does not result in complicated dependencies, rather the data model should be flexible enough so that changes in the business can be implemented within the data model in a relatively quick and efficient way.

- Entity types are often not identified, or are identified incorrectly. This can lead to replication of data, data structure and functionality, together with the attendant costs of that duplication in development and maintenance. Therefore, data definitions should be made as explicit and easy to understand as possible to minimize misinterpretation and duplication.

- Data models for different systems are arbitrarily different. The result of this is that complex interfaces are required between systems that share data. These interfaces can account for between 25-70% of the cost of current systems. Required interfaces should be considered inherently while designing a data model, as a data model on its own would not be usable without interfaces within different systems.

- Data cannot be shared electronically with customers and suppliers, because the structure and meaning of data has not been standardized. To obtain optimal value from an implemented data model, it is very important to define standards that will ensure that data models will both meet business needs and be consistent.

Conceptual, Logical and Physical Schemas

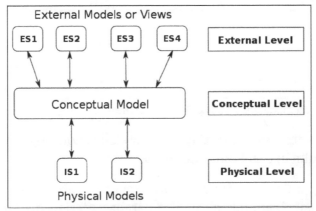

The ANSI/SPARC three level architecture: This shows that a data model can be an external model (or view), a conceptual model, or a physical model. This is not the only way to look at data models, but it is a useful way, particularly when comparing models.

In 1975 ANSI described three kinds of data-model instance:

- Conceptual schema: Describes the semantics of a domain (the scope of the model). For example, it may be a model of the interest area of an organization or of an industry. This consists of entity classes, representing kinds of things of significance in the domain, and relationships assertions about associations between pairs of entity classes. A conceptual schema specifies the kinds of facts or propositions that can be expressed using the model. In that sense, it defines the allowed expressions in an artificial "language" with a scope that is limited by the scope of the model. Simply described, a conceptual schema is the first step in organizing the data requirements.

- Logical schema: Describes the structure of some domain of information. This consists of descriptions of (for example) tables, columns, object-oriented classes, and XML tags. The logical schema and conceptual schema are sometimes implemented as one and the same.

- Physical schema: Describes the physical means used to store data. This is concerned with partitions, CPUs, tablespaces, and the like.

According to ANSI, this approach allows the three perspectives to be relatively independent of each other. Storage technology can change without affecting either the logical or the conceptual schema. The table/column structure can change without (necessarily) affecting the conceptual schema. In each case, of course, the structures must remain consistent across all schemas of the same data model.

Data Modeling Process

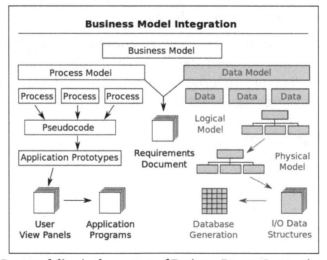

Data modeling in the context of Business Process Integration.

In the context of business process integration, data modeling complements business process modeling, and ultimately results in database generation.

The process of designing a database involves producing the previously described three types of schemas - conceptual, logical, and physical. The database design documented in these schemas is converted through a Data Definition Language, which can then be used to generate a database. A fully attributed data model contains detailed attributes (descriptions) for every entity within it.

The term "database design" can describe many different parts of the design of an overall database system. Principally, and most correctly, it can be thought of as the logical design of the base data structures used to store the data. In the relational model these are the tables and views. In an object database the entities and relationships map directly to object classes and named relationships. However, the term "database design" could also be used to apply to the overall process of designing, not just the base data structures, but also the forms and queries used as part of the overall database application within the Database Management System or DBMS.

In the process, system interfaces account for 25% to 70% of the development and support costs of current systems. The primary reason for this cost is that these systems do not share a common data model. If data models are developed on a system by system basis, then not only is the same analysis repeated in overlapping areas, but further analysis must be performed to create the interfaces between them. Most systems within an organization contain the same basic data, redeveloped for a specific purpose. Therefore, an efficiently designed basic data model can minimize rework with minimal modifications for the purposes of different systems within the organization

Modeling Methodologies

Data models represent information areas of interest. While there are many ways to create data models, according to Len Silverston only two modeling methodologies stand out, top-down and bottom-up:

- Bottom-up models or View Integration models are often the result of a reengineering effort. They usually start with existing data structures forms, fields on application screens, or reports. These models are usually physical, application-specific, and incomplete from an enterprise perspective. They may not promote data sharing, especially if they are built without reference to other parts of the organization.

- Top-down logical data models, on the other hand, are created in an abstract way by getting information from people who know the subject area. A system may not implement all the entities in a logical model, but the model serves as a reference point or template.

Sometimes models are created in a mixture of the two methods: by considering the data needs and structure of an application and by consistently referencing a subject-area model. Unfortunately, in many environments the distinction between a logical data model and a physical data model is blurred. In addition, some CASE tools don't make a distinction between logical and physical data models.

Entity Relationship Diagrams

There are several notations for data modeling. The actual model is frequently called "Entity relationship model", because it depicts data in terms of the entities and relationships described in the data. An entity-relationship model (ERM) is an abstract conceptual representation of structured data. Entity-relationship modeling is a relational schema database modeling method, used in software engineering to produce a type of conceptual data model (or semantic data model) of a system, often a relational database, and its requirements in a top-down fashion.

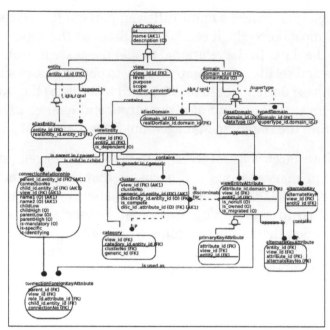

Example of an IDEF1X Entity relationship diagrams used to model IDEF1X itself.
The name of the view is mm. The domain hierarchy and constraints are also given.
The constraints are expressed as sentences in the formal theory of the meta model.

These models are being used in the first stage of information system design during the requirements analysis to describe information needs or the type of information that is to be stored in a database. The data modeling technique can be used to describe any ontology (i.e. an overview and classifications of used terms and their relationships) for a certain universe of discourse i.e. area of interest.

Several techniques have been developed for the design of data models. While these methodologies guide data modelers in their work, two different people using the same methodology will often come up with very different results.

- Bachman diagrams

- Barker's notation

- Chen's Notation

- Data Vault Modeling

- Extended Backus–Naur form

- IDEF1X

- Object-relational mapping

- Object-Role Modeling

- Relational Model

- Relational Model/Tasmania

Generic Data Modeling

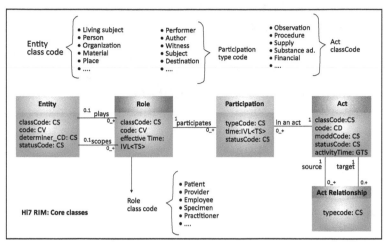

Example of a Generic data model.

Generic data models are generalizations of conventional data models. They define standardized general relation types, together with the kinds of things that may be related by such a relation type. The definition of generic data model is similar to the definition of a natural language. For example, a generic data model may define relation types such as a 'classification relation', being a binary relation between an individual thing and a kind of thing (a class) and a 'part-whole relation', being a binary relation between two things, one with the role of part, the other with the role of whole, regardless the kind of things that are related.

Given an extensible list of classes, this allows the classification of any individual thing and to specify part-whole relations for any individual object. By standardization of an extensible list of relation types, a generic data model enables the expression of an unlimited number of kinds of facts and will approach the capabilities of natural languages. Conventional data models, on the other hand, have a fixed and limited domain scope, because the instantiation (usage) of such a model only allows expressions of kinds of facts that are predefined in the model.

Semantic Data Modeling

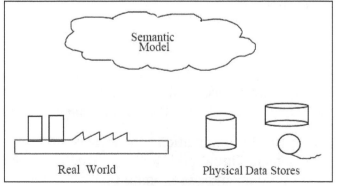

Semantic data models

The logical data structure of a DBMS, whether hierarchical, network, or relational, cannot totally satisfy the requirements for a conceptual definition of data because it is limited in scope and biased toward the implementation strategy employed by the DBMS. That is unless the semantic data model is implemented in the database on purpose, a choice which may slightly impact performance but generally vastly improves productivity.

Therefore, the need to define data from a conceptual view has led to the development of semantic data modeling techniques. That is, techniques to define the meaning of data within the context of its interrelationships with other data. As illustrated in the figure the real world, in terms of resources, ideas, events, etc., are symbolically defined within physical data stores. A semantic data model is an abstraction which defines how the stored symbols relate to the real world. Thus, the model must be a true representation of the real world.

A semantic data model can be used to serve many purposes, such as:

- Planning of data resources

- Building of shareable databases

- Evaluation of vendor software

- Integration of existing databases

The overall goal of semantic data models is to capture more meaning of data by integrating relational concepts with more powerful abstraction concepts known from the Artificial Intelligence field. The idea is to provide high level modeling primitives as integral part of a data model in order to facilitate the representation of real world situations.

CONTINUOUS INTEGRATION

In software engineering, continuous integration (CI) is the practice of merging all developers' working copies to a shared mainline several times a day. Grady Booch first proposed the term CI in his 1991 method, although he did not advocate integrating several times a day. Extreme programming (XP) adopted the concept of CI and did advocate integrating more than once per day – perhaps as many as tens of times per day.

Rationale

The main aim of CI is to prevent integration problems, referred to as "integration hell" in early descriptions of XP. CI is not universally accepted as an improvement over frequent integration, so it is important to distinguish between the two as there is disagreement about the virtues of each.

In XP, CI was intended to be used in combination with automated unit tests written through the practices of test-driven development. Initially this was conceived of as running and passing all unit tests in the developer's local environment before committing to the mainline. This helps avoid one developer's work-in-progress breaking another developer's copy. Where necessary, partially complete features can be disabled before committing, using feature toggles for instance.

Later elaborations of the concept introduced build servers, which automatically ran the unit tests periodically or even after every commit and reported the results to the developers. The use of build servers (not necessarily running unit tests) had already been practised by some teams outside the XP community. Nowadays, many organisations have adopted CI without adopting all of XP.

In addition to automated unit tests, organisations using CI typically use a build server to implement *continuous* processes of applying quality control in general — small pieces of effort, applied frequently. In addition to running the unit and integration tests, such processes run additional static and dynamic tests, measure and profile performance, extract and format documentation from the source code and facilitate manual QA processes. This continuous application of quality control aims to improve the quality of software, and to reduce the time taken to deliver it, by replacing the traditional practice of applying quality control *after* completing all development. This is very similar to the original idea of integrating more frequently to make integration easier, only applied to QA processes.

In the same vein, the practice of continuous delivery further extends CI by making sure the software checked in on the mainline is always in a state that can be deployed to users and makes the deployment process very rapid.

Workflow

When embarking on a change, a developer takes a copy of the current code base on which to work. As other developers submit changed code to the source code repository, this copy gradually ceases to reflect the repository code. Not only can the existing code base change, but new code can be added as well as new libraries, and other resources that create dependencies, and potential conflicts.

The longer development continues on a branch without merging back to the mainline, the greater the risk of multiple integration conflicts and failures when the developer branch is eventually merged back. When developers submit code to the repository they must first update their code to reflect the changes in the repository since they took their copy. The more changes the repository contains, the more work developers must do before submitting their own changes.

Eventually, the repository may become so different from the developers' baselines that they enter what is sometimes referred to as "merge hell", or "integration hell", where the time it takes to integrate exceeds the time it took to make their original changes.

Continuous integration involves integrating early and often, so as to avoid the pitfalls of "integration hell". The practice aims to reduce rework and thus reduce cost and time. A complementary practice to CI is that before submitting work, each programmer must do a complete build and run (and pass) all unit tests. Integration tests are usually run automatically on a CI server when it detects a new commit.

Common Practices

Continuous integration – the practice of frequently integrating one's new or changed code with the existing code repository – should occur frequently enough that no intervening window remains between commit and build, and such that no errors can arise without developers noticing them and correcting them immediately. Normal practice is to trigger these builds by every commit to a repository, rather than a periodically scheduled build. The practicalities of doing this in a multi-developer environment of rapid commits are such that it is usual to trigger a short time after each commit, then to start a build when either this timer expires, or after a rather longer interval since the last build. Note that since each new commit resets the timer used for the short time trigger, this is the same technique used in many button debouncing algorithms [ex:]. In this way the commit events are "denounced" to prevent unnecessary builds between a series of rapid-fire commits. Many automated tools offer this scheduling automatically.

Another factor is the need for a version control system that supports atomic commits, i.e. all of a developer's changes may be seen as a single commit operation. There is no point in trying to build from only half of the changed files. To achieve these objectives, continuous integration relies on the following principles.

Maintain a Code Repository

This practice advocates the use of a revision control system for the project's source code. All artifacts required to build the project should be placed in the repository. In this practice and in the revision control community, the convention is that the system should be buildable from a fresh checkout and not require additional dependencies. Extreme Programming advocate Martin Fowler also mentions that where branching is supported by tools, its use should be minimised. Instead, it is preferred for changes to be integrated rather than for multiple versions of the software to be maintained simultaneously. The mainline (or trunk) should be the place for the working version of the software.

Automate the Build

A single command should have the capability of building the system. Many build tools, such as make, have existed for many years. Other more recent tools are frequently used in continuous integration environments. Automation of the build should include automating the integration, which often includes deployment into a production-like environment. In many cases, the build script not only compiles binaries, but also generates documentation, website pages, statistics and distribution media (such as Debian DEB, Red Hat RPM or Windows MSI files).

Make the Build Self-testing

Once the code is built, all tests should run to confirm that it behaves as the developers expect it to behave.

Everyone Commits to the Baseline Every Day

By committing regularly, every committer can reduce the number of conflicting changes. Checking in a week's worth of work runs the risk of conflicting with other features and can be very difficult to resolve. Early, small conflicts in an area of the system cause team members to communicate about the change they are making. Committing all changes at least once a day (once per feature built) is generally considered part of the definition of Continuous Integration. In addition performing a nightly build is generally recommended. These are lower bounds; the typical frequency is expected to be much higher.

Every Commit (to Baseline) should be Built

The system should build commits to the current working version to verify that they integrate correctly. A common practice is to use Automated Continuous Integration, although this may be done manually. Automated Continuous Integration employs a continuous integration server or daemon to monitor the revision control system for changes, then automatically run the build process.

Keep the Build Fast

The build needs to complete rapidly, so that if there is a problem with integration, it is quickly identified.

Test in a Clone of the Production Environment

Having a test environment can lead to failures in tested systems when they deploy in the production environment because the production environment may differ from the test environment in a significant way. However, building a replica of a production environment is cost prohibitive. Instead, the test environment, or a separate pre-production environment ("staging") should be built to be a scalable version of the production environment to alleviate costs while maintaining technology stack composition and nuances. Within these test environments, service virtualisation is commonly used to obtain on-demand access to dependencies (e.g., APIs, third-party applications, services, mainframes, etc.) that are beyond the team's control, still evolving, or too complex to configure in a virtual test lab.

Make it Easy to Get the Latest Deliverables

Making builds readily available to stakeholders and testers can reduce the amount of rework necessary when rebuilding a feature that doesn't meet requirements. Additionally, early testing reduces the chances that defects survive until deployment. Finding errors earlier can reduce the amount of work necessary to resolve them.

All programmers should start the day by updating the project from the repository. That way, they will all stay up to date.

Everyone can see the Results of the Latest Build

It should be easy to find out whether the build breaks and, if so, who made the relevant change and what that change was.

Automate Deployment

Most CI systems allow the running of scripts after a build finishes. In most situations, it is possible to write a script to deploy the application to a live test server that everyone can look at. A further advance in this way of thinking is continuous deployment, which calls for the software to be deployed directly into production, often with additional automation to prevent defects or regressions.

Costs and Benefits

Continuous integration is intended to produce benefits such as:

- Integration bugs are detected early and are easy to track down due to small change sets. This saves both time and money over the lifespan of a project.

- Avoids last-minute chaos at release dates, when everyone tries to check in their slightly incompatible versions.

- When unit tests fail or a bug emerges, if developers need to revert the codebase to a bug-free state without debugging, only a small number of changes are lost (because integration happens frequently).

- Constant availability of a "current" build for testing, demo, or release purposes.

- Frequent code check-in pushes developers to create modular, less complex code.

With continuous automated testing benefits can include:

- Enforces discipline of frequent automated testing.

- Immediate feedback on system-wide impact of local changes.

- Software metrics generated from automated testing and CI (such as metrics for code coverage, code complexity, and feature completeness) focus developers on developing functional, quality code, and help develop momentum in a team.

Some downsides of continuous integration can include:

- Constructing an automated test suite requires a considerable amount of work, including ongoing effort to cover new features and follow intentional code modifications.

  - Testing is considered a best practice for software development in its own right, regardless of whether or not continuous integration is employed, and automation is an integral part of project methodologies like test-driven development.

  - Continuous integration can be performed without any test suite, but the cost of quality assurance to produce a releasable product can be high if it must be done manually and frequently.

- There is some work involved to set up a build system, and it can become complex, making it difficult to modify flexibly.

  - However, there are a number of continuous integration software projects, both proprietary and open-source, which can be used.

- Continuous Integration is not necessarily valuable if the scope of the project is small or contains untestable legacy code.

- Value added depends on the quality of tests and how testable the code really is.

- Larger teams means that new code is constantly added to the integration queue, so tracking deliveries (while preserving quality) is difficult and builds queueing up can slow down everyone.

- With multiple commits and merges a day, partial code for a feature could easily be pushed and therefore integration tests will fail until the feature is complete.

- Safety and mission-critical development assurance. require rigorous documentation and in-process review that are difficult to achieve using Continuous Integration. This type of life cycle often requires additional steps be completed prior to product release when regulatory approval of the product is required.

SOFTWARE ARCHITECTURE

Software architecture refers to the fundamental structures of a software system and the discipline of creating such structures and systems. Each structure comprises software elements, relations among them, and properties of both elements and relations. The *architecture* of a software system is a metaphor, analogous to the architecture of a building. It functions as a blueprint for the system and the developing project, laying out the tasks not necessary to be executed by the design teams.

Software architecture is about making fundamental structural choices that are costly to change once implemented. Software architecture choices include specific structural options from possibilities in the design of software. For example, the systems that controlled the space shuttle launch vehicle had the requirement of being very fast and very reliable. Therefore, an appropriate real-time computing language would need to be chosen. Additionally, to satisfy the need for reliability the choice could be made to have multiple redundant and independently produced copies of the program, and to run these copies on independent hardware while cross-checking results.

Documenting software architecture facilitates communication between stakeholders, captures early decisions about the high-level design, and allows reuse of design components between projects.

Scope

Opinions vary as to the scope of software architectures:

- Overall, macroscopic system structure; this refers to architecture as a higher level abstraction of a software system that consists of a collection of computational components together with connectors that describe the interaction between these components.

- The important stuff—whatever that is; this refers to the fact that software architects should concern themselves with those decisions that have high impact on the system and its stakeholders.

- That which is fundamental to understanding a system in its environment".

- Things that people perceive as hard to change; since designing the architecture takes place at the beginning of a software system's lifecycle, the architect should focus on decisions that "have to" be right the first time. Following this line of thought, architectural design issues may become non-architectural once their irreversibility can be overcome.

- A set of architectural design decisions; software architecture should not be considered merely a set of models or structures, but should include the decisions that lead to these particular structures, and the rationale behind them. This insight has led to substantial research into software architecture knowledge management.

There is no sharp distinction between software architecture versus design and requirements engineering. They are all part of a "chain of intentionality" from high-level intentions to low-level details.

Characteristics

Software architecture exhibits the following:

1. Multitude of stakeholders: Software systems have to cater to a variety of stakeholders such as business managers, owners, users, and operators. These stakeholders all have their own concerns with respect to the system. Balancing these concerns and demonstrating how they are addressed is part of designing the system. This implies that architecture involves dealing with a broad variety of concerns and stakeholders, and has a multidisciplinary nature.

2. Separation of concerns: The established way for architects to reduce complexity is to separate the concerns that drive the design. Architecture documentation shows that all stakeholder concerns are addressed by modeling and describing the architecture from separate points of view associated with the various stakeholder concerns. These separate descriptions are called architectural.

3. Quality-driven: Classic software design approaches (e.g. Jackson Structured Programming) were driven by required functionality and the flow of data through the system, but the current insight is that the architecture of a software system is more closely related to its quality attributes such as fault-tolerance, backward compatibility, extensibility, reliability, maintainability, availability, security, usability, and other such –ilities. Stakeholder concerns often translate into requirements on these quality attributes, which are variously called non-functional requirements, extra-functional requirements, behavioral requirements, or quality attribute requirements.

4. Recurring styles: Like building architecture, the software architecture discipline has developed standard ways to address recurring concerns. These "standard ways" are called by various names at various levels of abstraction. Common terms for recurring solutions are architectural style, tactic, reference architecture and architectural pattern.

5. Conceptual integrity: A term introduced by Fred Brooks in *The Mythical Man-Month* to denote the idea that the architecture of a software system represents an overall vision of what it should do and how it should do it. This vision should be separated from its implementation. The architect assumes the role of "keeper of the vision", making sure that additions to the system are in line with the architecture, hence preserving conceptual integrity.

6. Cognitive constraints: An observation first made in a 1967 paper by computer programmer Melvin Conway that organizations which design systems are constrained to produce designs which are copies of the communication structures of these organizations.

Motivation

Software architecture is an "intellectually graspable" abstraction of a complex system. This abstraction provides a number of benefits:

- It gives a basis for analysis of software systems' behavior before the system has been built. The ability to verify that a future software system fulfills its stakeholders' needs without actually having to build it represents substantial cost-saving and risk-mitigation. A number of techniques have been developed to perform such analyses, such as ATAM.

- It provides a basis for re-use of elements and decisions. A complete software architecture or parts of it, like individual architectural strategies and decisions, can be re-used across multiple systems whose stakeholders require similar quality attributes or functionality, saving design costs and mitigating the risk of design mistakes.

- It supports early design decisions that impact a system's development, deployment, and maintenance life. Getting the early, high-impact decisions right is important to prevent schedule and budget overruns.

- It facilitates communication with stakeholders, contributing to a system that better fulfills their needs. Communicating about complex systems from the point of view of stakeholders helps them understand the consequences of their stated requirements and the design decisions based on them. Architecture gives the ability to communicate about design decisions before the system is implemented, when they are still relatively easy to adapt.

- It helps in risk management. Software architecture helps to reduce risks and chance of failure.

- It enables cost reduction. Software architecture is a means to manage risk and costs in complex IT projects.

Architecture Activities

There are many activities that a software architect performs. A software architect typically works with project managers, discusses architecturally significant requirements with stakeholders, designs a software architecture, evaluates a design, communicates with designers and stakeholders, documents the architectural design and more. There are four core activities in software architecture design. These core architecture activities are performed iteratively and at different stages of the initial software development life-cycle, as well as over the evolution of a system.

Architectural analysis is the process of understanding the environment in which a proposed system or systems will operate and determining the requirements for the system. The input or requirements to the analysis activity can come from any number of stakeholders and include items such as:

- What the system will do when operational (the functional requirements).

- How well the system will perform runtime non-functional requirements such as reliability, operability, performance efficiency, security, compatibility defined in iso/iec 25010:2011 standard.

- Development-time non-functional requirements such as maintainability and transferability defined in iso 25010:2011 standard.

- Business requirements and environmental contexts of a system that may change over time, such as legal, social, financial, competitive, and technology concerns.

The outputs of the analysis activity are those requirements that have a measurable impact on a software system's architecture, called architecturally significant requirements.

Architectural synthesis or design is the process of creating architecture. Given the architecturally significant requirements determined by the analysis, the current state of the design and the results of any evaluation activities, the design is created and improved.

Architecture evaluation is the process of determining how well the current design or a portion of it satisfies the requirements derived during analysis. An evaluation can occur whenever an architect is considering a design decision, it can occur after some portion of the design has been completed, it can occur after the final design has been completed or it can occur after the system has been constructed. Some of the available software architecture evaluation techniques include Architecture Tradeoff Analysis Method (ATAM) and TARA. Frameworks for comparing the techniques are discussed in frameworks such as *SARA Report* and *Architecture Reviews: Practice and Experience*.

Architecture evolution is the process of maintaining and adapting an existing software architecture to meet changes in requirements and environment. As software architecture provides a fundamental structure of a software system, its evolution and maintenance would necessarily impact its fundamental structure. As such, architecture evolution is concerned with adding new functionality as well as maintaining existing functionality and system behavior.

Architecture requires critical supporting activities. These supporting activities take place throughout the core software architecture process. They include knowledge management and communication, design reasoning and decision making, and documentation.

Architecture Supporting Activities

Software architecture supporting activities are carried out during core software architecture activities. These supporting activities assist a software architect to carry out analysis, synthesis, evaluation, and evolution. For instance, an architect has to gather knowledge, make decisions and document during the analysis phase.

- Knowledge management and communication is the act of exploring and managing knowledge that is essential to designing a software architecture. A software architect does not work in isolation. They get inputs, functional and non-functional requirements and design contexts, from various stakeholders; and provides outputs to stakeholders. Software architecture knowledge is often tacit and is retained in the heads of stakeholders. Software architecture knowledge management activity is about finding, communicating, and retaining knowledge. As software architecture design issues are intricate and interdependent, a knowledge gap in design reasoning can lead to incorrect software architecture design.

- Design reasoning and decision making is the activity of evaluating design decisions. This activity is fundamental to all three core software architecture activities. It entails gathering and associating decision contexts, formulating design decision problems, finding solution options and evaluating tradeoffs before making decisions. This process occurs at different levels of decision granularity while evaluating significant architectural requirements and software architecture decisions, and software architecture analysis, synthesis, and evaluation. Examples of reasoning activities include understanding the impacts of a requirement or a design on quality attributes, questioning the issues that a design might cause, assessing possible solution options, and evaluating the tradeoffs between solutions.

- Documentation is the act of recording the design generated during the software architecture process. A system design is described using several views that frequently include a static view showing the code structure of the system, a dynamic view showing the actions of the system during execution, and a deployment view showing how a system is placed on hardware for execution. Documenting Software Architectures: Views and Beyond has descriptions of the kinds of notations that could be used within the view description. Examples of documentation activities are writing a specification, recording a system design model, documenting a design rationale, developing a viewpoint, documenting views.

Software Architecture Topics

Software Architecture Description

Software architecture description involves the principles and practices of modeling and representing architectures, using mechanisms such as: architecture description languages, architecture viewpoints, and architecture frameworks.

Architecture Description Languages

An architecture description language (ADL) is any means of expression used to describe a software architecture (ISO/IEC/IEEE 42010). Many special-purpose ADLs have been developed since the 1990s, including AADL (SAE standard).

Architecture Viewpoints

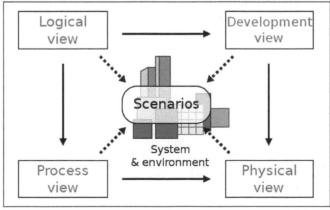

4+1 Architectural View Model.

Software architecture descriptions are commonly organized into views, which are analogous to the different types of blueprints made in building architecture. Each view addresses a set of system concerns, following the conventions of its *viewpoint*, where a viewpoint is a specification that describes the notations, modeling, and analysis techniques to use in a view that express the architecture in question from the perspective of a given set of stakeholders and their concerns (ISO/IEC/IEEE 42010). The viewpoint specifies not only the concerns framed (i.e., to be addressed) but the presentation, model kinds used, conventions used and any consistency (correspondence) rules to keep a view consistent with other views.

Architecture Frameworks

An architecture framework captures the "conventions, principles and practices for the description of architectures established within a specific domain of application and/or community of stakeholders" (ISO/IEC/IEEE 42010). A framework is usually implemented in terms of one or more viewpoints or ADLs.

Architectural Styles and Patterns

An architectural pattern is a general, reusable solution to a commonly occurring problem in software architecture within a given context. Architectural patterns are often documented as software design patterns.

Following traditional building architecture, a 'software architectural style' is a specific method of construction, characterized by the features that make it notable" (architectural style).

There are many recognized architectural patterns and styles, among them:

- Blackboard
- Client-server (2-tier, 3-tier, n-tier, cloud computing exhibit this style)
- Component-based
- Data-centric
- Event-driven (or implicit invocation)
- Layered (or multilayered architecture)
- Microservices architecture
- Monolithic application
- Peer-to-peer (P2P)
- Pipes and filters
- Plug-ins
- Representational state transfer (REST)
- Rule-based
- Service-oriented

- Shared nothing architecture

- Space-based architecture

Some treat architectural patterns and architectural styles as the same, some treat styles as specializations of patterns. What they have in common is both patterns and styles are idioms for architects to use, they "provide a common language" or "vocabulary" with which to describe classes of systems.

Software Architecture and Agile Development

There are also concerns that software architecture leads to too much Big Design Up Front, especially among proponents of agile software development. A number of methods have been developed to balance the trade-offs of up-front design and agility, including the agile method DSDM which mandates a "Foundations" phase during which "just enough" architectural foundations are laid. IEEE Software devoted a special issue to the interaction between agility and architecture.

Software Architecture Erosion

Software architecture erosion (or "decay") refers to the gap observed between the planned and actual architecture of a software system as realized in its implementation. Software architecture erosion occurs when implementation decisions either do not fully achieve the architecture-as-planned or otherwise violate constraints or principles of that architecture. The gap between planned and actual architectures is sometimes understood in terms of the notion of technical debt.

As an example, consider a strictly layered system, where each layer can only use services provided by the layer immediately below it. Any source code component that does not observe this constraint represents an architecture violation. If not corrected, such violations can transform the architecture into a monolithic block, with adverse effects on understandability, maintainability, and evolvability.

Various approaches have been proposed to address erosion. "These approaches, which include tools, techniques, and processes, are primarily classified into three general categories that attempt to minimize, prevent and repair architecture erosion. Within these broad categories, each approach is further broken down reflecting the high-level strategies adopted to tackle erosion. These are process-oriented architecture conformance, architecture evolution management, architecture design enforcement, architecture to implementation linkage, self-adaptation and architecture restoration techniques consisting of recovery, discovery, and reconciliation."

There are two major techniques to detect architectural violations: reflexion models and domain-specific languages. Reflexion model (RM) techniques compare a high-level model provided by the system's architects with the source code implementation. There are also domain-specific languages with a focus on specifying and checking architectural constraints.

Software Architecture Recovery

Software architecture recovery (or reconstruction, or reverse engineering) includes the methods, techniques, and processes to uncover a software system's architecture from available information, including its implementation and documentation. Architecture recovery is often necessary to make informed decisions in the face of obsolete or out-of-date documentation and architecture erosion: implementation and maintenance decisions diverging from the envisioned architecture. Practices exist to recover software architecture as Static program analysis. This is a part of subjects covered by the Software intelligence practice.

Related Fields

Design

Architecture is design but not all design is architectural. In practice, the architect is the one who draws the line between software architecture (architectural design) and detailed design (non-architectural design). There are no rules or guidelines that fit all cases, although there have been attempts to formalize the distinction. According to the *Intension/Locality Hypothesis*, the distinction between architectural and detailed design is defined by the *Locality Criterion*, according to which a statement about software design is non-local (architectural) if and only if a program that satisfies it can be expanded into a program that does not. For example, the client–server style is architectural (strategic) because a program that is built on this principle can be expanded into a program that is not client–server—for example, by adding peer-to-peer nodes.

Requirements Engineering

Requirements engineering and software architecture can be seen as complementary approaches: while software architecture targets the 'solution space' or the 'how', requirements engineering addresses the 'problem space' or the 'what'. Requirements engineering entails the elicitation, negotiation, specification, validation, documentation and management of requirements. Both requirements engineering and software architecture revolve around stakeholder concerns, needs and wishes.

There is considerable overlap between requirements engineering and software architecture, as evidenced for example by a study into five industrial software architecture methods that concludes that "the inputs (goals, constraints, etc.) are usually ill-defined, and only get discovered or better understood as the architecture starts to emerge" and that while "most architectural concerns are expressed as requirements on the system, they can also include mandated design decisions". In short, the choice of required behavior given a particular problem impacts the architecture of the solution that addresses that problem, while at the same time the architectural design may impact the problem and introduce new requirements. Approaches such as the Twin Peaks model aim to exploit the synergistic relation between requirements and architecture.

Other Types of Architecture

1. Computer architecture: Computer architecture targets the internal structure of a computer system, in terms of collaborating hardware components such as the CPU – or processor – the bus and the memory.

2. Systems architecture: The term systems architecture has originally been applied to the architecture of systems that consists of both hardware and software. The main concern addressed by the systems architecture is then the integration of software and hardware in a

complete, correctly working device. In another common – much broader – meaning, the term applies to the architecture of any complex system which may be of technical, socio-technical or social nature.

3. Enterprise architecture: The goal of enterprise architecture is to "translate business vision and strategy into effective enterprise". Enterprise architecture frameworks, such as TOGAF and the Zachman Framework, usually distinguish between different enterprise architecture layers. Although terminology differs from framework to framework, many include at least a distinction between a *business layer*, an *application* (or *information*) *layer*, and a *technology layer*. Enterprise architecture addresses among others the alignment between these layers, usually in a top-down approach.

COUPLING

In software engineering, coupling is the degree of interdependence between software modules; a measure of how closely connected two routines or modules are; the strength of the relationships between modules.

Coupling is usually contrasted with cohesion. Low coupling often correlates with high cohesion, and vice versa. Low coupling is often a sign of a well-structured [computer system] and a good design, and when combined with high cohesion, supports the general goals of high readability and maintainability.

Types of Coupling

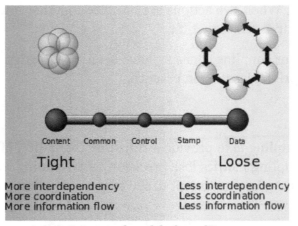

Conceptual model of coupling.

Coupling can be "low" (also "loose" and "weak") or "high" (also "tight" and "strong"). Some types of coupling, in order of highest to lowest coupling, are as follows:

Procedural Programming

A module here refers to a subroutine of any kind, i.e. a set of one or more statements having a name and preferably its own set of variable names.

1. Content coupling (high): Content coupling is said to occur when one module uses the code of other module, for instance a branch. This violates information hiding - a basic design concept.

2. Common coupling: Common coupling is said to occur when several modules have access to the same global data. But it can lead to uncontrolled error propagation and unforeseen side-effects when changes are made.

3. External coupling: External coupling occurs when two modules share an externally imposed data format, communication protocol, or device interface. This is basically related to the communication to external tools and devices.

4. Control coupling: Control coupling is one module controlling the flow of another, by passing it information on what to do (e.g., passing a what-to-do flag).

5. Stamp coupling (data-structured coupling): Stamp coupling occurs when modules share a composite data structure and use only parts of it, possibly different parts (e.g., passing a whole record to a function that needs only one field of it). In this situation, a modification in a field that a module does not need may lead to changing the way the module reads the record.

6. Data coupling: Data coupling occurs when modules share data through, for example, parameters. Each datum is an elementary piece, and these are the only data shared (e.g., passing an integer to a function that computes a square root).

Object-oriented Programming

- Subclass coupling: Describes the relationship between a child and its parent. The child is connected to its parent, but the parent is not connected to the child.

- Temporal coupling: When two actions are bundled together into one module just because they happen to occur at the same time.

In recent work various other coupling concepts have been investigated and used as indicators for different modularization principles used in practice.

Dynamic Coupling

The goal of this type of coupling is to provide a run-time evaluation of a software system. It has been argued that static coupling metrics lose precision when dealing with an intensive use of dynamic binding or inheritance . In the attempt to solve this issue, dynamic coupling measures have been taken into account.

Semantic Coupling

This kind of coupling considers the conceptual similarities between software entities using, for example, comments and identifiers and relying on techniques such as Latent Semantic Indexing (LSI).

Logical Coupling

Logical coupling (or evolutionary coupling or change coupling) exploits the release history of a software system to find change patterns among modules or classes: e.g., entities that are likely to be changed together or sequences of changes (a change in a class A is always followed by a change in a class B).

Disadvantages

Tightly coupled systems tend to exhibit the following developmental characteristics, which are often seen as disadvantages:

1. A change in one module usually forces a ripple effect of changes in other modules.

2. Assembly of modules might require more effort and/or time due to the increased inter-module dependency.

3. A particular module might be harder to reuse and/or test because dependent modules must be included.

Performance Issues

Whether loosely or tightly coupled, a system's performance is often reduced by message and parameter creation, transmission, translation (e.g. marshaling) and message interpretation (which might be a reference to a string, array or data structure), which require less overhead than creating a complicated message such as a SOAP message. Longer messages require more CPU and memory to produce. To optimize runtime performance, message length must be minimized and message meaning must be maximized.

1. Message Transmission Overhead and Performance: Since a message must be transmitted in full to retain its complete meaning, message transmission must be optimized. Longer messages require more CPU and memory to transmit and receive. Also, when necessary, receivers must reassemble a message into its original state to completely receive it. Hence, to optimize runtime performance, message length must be minimized and message meaning must be maximized.

2. Message Translation Overhead and Performance: Message protocols and messages themselves often contain extra information (i.e., packet, structure, definition and language information). Hence, the receiver often needs to translate a message into a more refined form by removing extra characters and structure information and/or by converting values from one type to another. Any sort of translation increases CPU and/or memory overhead. To optimize runtime performance, message form and content must be reduced and refined to maximize its meaning and reduce translation.

3. Message Interpretation Overhead and Performance: All messages must be interpreted by the receiver. Simple messages such as integers might not require additional processing to be interpreted. However, complex messages such as SOAP messages require a parser and a string transformer for them to exhibit intended meanings. To optimize runtime performance, messages must be refined and reduced to minimize interpretation overhead.

Solutions

One approach to decreasing coupling is functional design, which seeks to limit the responsibilities of modules along functionality. Coupling increases between two classes A and B if:

- A has an attribute that refers to (is of type) B.

- *A* calls on services of an object *B*.

- *A* has a method that references *B* (via return type or parameter).

- *A* is a subclass of (or implements) class *B*.

Low coupling refers to a relationship in which one module interacts with another module through a simple and stable interface and does not need to be concerned with the other module's internal implementation.

Systems such as CORBA or COM allow objects to communicate with each other without having to know anything about the other object's implementation. Both of these systems even allow for objects to communicate with objects written in other languages.

Coupling versus Cohesion

Coupling and cohesion are terms which occur together very frequently. Coupling refers to the interdependencies between modules, while cohesion describes how related the functions within a single module are. Low cohesion implies that a given module performs tasks which are not very related to each other and hence can create problems as the module becomes large.

Module Coupling

Coupling in Software Engineering describes a version of metrics associated with this concept.

For data and control flow coupling:

- d_i: number of input data parameters.

- c_i: number of input control parameters.

- d_o: number of output data parameters.

- c_o: number of output control parameters.

For global coupling:

- g_d: number of global variables used as data.

- g_c: number of global variables used as control.

For environmental coupling:

- w: number of modules called (fan-out).

- r: number of modules calling the module under consideration (fan-in).

$$\text{Coupling}(C) = 1 - \frac{1}{d_i + 2 \times c_i + d_o + 2 \times c_o + g_d + 2 \times g_c + w + r}$$

`Coupling(C)` makes the value larger the more coupled the module is. This number ranges from approximately 0.67 (low coupling) to 1.0 (highly coupled). For example, if a module has only a single input and output data parameter:

$$C = 1 - \frac{1}{1+0+1+0+0+0+1+0} = 1 - \frac{1}{3} = 0.67$$

If a module has 5 input and output data parameters, an equal number of control parameters, and accesses 10 items of global data, with a fan-in of 3 and a fan-out of 4:

$$C = 1 - \frac{1}{5+2\times5+5+2\times5+10+0+3+4} = 0.98.$$

DEBUGGING

In the context of software engineering, debugging is the process of fixing a bug in the software. In other words, it refers to identifying, analyzing and removing errors. This activity begins after the software fails to execute properly and concludes by solving the problem and successfully testing the software. It is considered to be an extremely complex and tedious task because errors need to be resolved at all stages of debugging.

Debugging Process: Steps involved in debugging are:

- Problem identification and report preparation.
- Assigning the report to software engineer to the defect to verify that it is genuine.
- Defect Analysis using modeling, documentations, finding and testing candidate flaws, etc.
- Defect Resolution by making required changes to the system.
- Validation of corrections.

Debugging Strategies

1. Study the system for the larger duration in order to understand the system. It helps debugger to construct different representations of systems to be debugging depends on the need. Study of the system is also done actively to find recent changes made to the software.

2. Backwards analysis of the problem which involves tracing the program backward from the location of failure message in order to identify the region of faulty code. A detailed study of the region is conducting to find the cause of defects.

3. Forward analysis of the program involves tracing the program forwards using breakpoints or print statements at different points in the program and studying the results. The region where the wrong outputs are obtained is the region that needs to be focused to find the defect.

4. Using the past experience of the software debug the software with similar problems in nature. The success of this approach depends on the expertise of the debugger.

Debugging Tools

Debugging tool is a computer program that is used to test and debug other programs. A lot of public domain software like gdb and dbx are available for debugging. They offer console-based command line interfaces. Examples of automated debugging tools include code based tracers, profilers, interpreters, etc.

Some of the widely used debuggers are:

- Radare2

- WinDbg

- Valgrind

Difference between Debugging and Testing

Debugging is different from testing. Testing focuses on finding bugs, errors, etc whereas debugging starts after a bug has been identified in the software. Testing is used to ensure that the program is correct and it was supposed to do with a certain minimum success rate. Testing can be manual or automated. There are several different types of testing like unit testing, integration testing, alpha and beta testing, etc. Debugging requires a lot of knowledge, skills, and expertise. It can be supported by some automated tools available but is more of a manual process as every bug is different and requires a different technique, unlike a pre-defined testing mechanism.

Need for Debugging

Once errors are known during a program code, it's necessary to initial establish the precise program statements liable for the errors and so to repair them. Debugging is the process of finding and resolving defects or problems within a computer program that prevent correct operation of computer software or a system.

Debugging Approaches

The following are a number of approaches popularly adopted by programmers for debugging.

- Brute Force Method: This is the foremost common technique of debugging however that is the least economical method during this approach. The program is loaded with print statements to print the intermediate values with the hope that a number of the written values can facilitate to spot the statement in error. This approach becomes a lot of systematic with the utilization of a symbolic program (also known as a source code debugger), as a result of values of various variables will be simply checked and breakpoints and watch points can be easily set to check the values of variables effortlessly.

- Backtracking: This is additionally a reasonably common approach during this approach, starting from the statement at which an error symptom has been discovered. The source code is derived backward till the error is discovered sadly, because the variety of supply lines to be derived back will increase, the quantity of potential backward methods will increase and should become unmanageably large so limiting the utilization of this approach.

- Cause Elimination Method: In this approach, a listing of causes that may presumably have contributed to the error symptom is developed and tests are conducted to eliminate every. A connected technique of identification of the error from the error symptom is that the package fault tree analysis.

- Program Slicing: This technique is analogous to backtracking. Here the search house is reduced by process slices. A slice of a program for a specific variable at a particular statement is that the set of supply lines preceding this statement which will influence the worth of that variable.

Debugging Guidelines

Debugging is commonly administrated by programmers supported their ingenuity. The subsequent are some general tips for effective debugging:

- Many times debugging needs an intensive understanding of the program style. Making an attempt to rectify supported a partial understanding of the system style and implementation might need an excessive quantity of effort to be placed into debugging even straightforward issues.

- Debugging might generally even need a full plan of the system. In such cases, a typical mistake that novice programmers usually create is trying to not fix the error however its symptoms.

- One should be watched out for the likelihood that a slip correction might introduce new errors. So when each spherical of error-fixing, regression testing should be administrated.

References

- Software-quality-assurance: softwaretestinghelp.com, Retrieved 20 April, 2019
- Software-engineering-debugging: geeksforgeeks.org, Retrieved 16 March, 2019
- Types-of-software-maintenance, software-engineering: ecomputernotes.com, Retrieved 14 May, 2019
- Software-engineering-debugging-approaches: geeksforgeeks.org, Retrieved 09 August, 2019

Software Development

The process of designing, conceiving, programming, specifying, documenting and testing applications is known as software development. Its purpose is to create and maintain different software components. All the diverse aspects of software development have been carefully analyzed in this chapter.

Software development is a process by which standalone or individual software is created using a specific programming language. It involves writing a series of interrelated programming code, which provides the functionality of the developed software. Software development may also be called application development and software design. Software development is an iterative logical process that aims to create a computer coded or programmed software to address a unique business or personal objective, goal or process. Software development is generally a planned initiative that consists of various steps or stages that result in the creation of operational software.

Software development is primarily achieved through computer programming, which is carried out by a software programmer and includes processes such as initial research, data flow design, process flow design, flow charts, technical documentation, software testing, debugging and other software architecture techniques. This is known as the software development life cycle (SDLC).

SOFTWARE DEVELOPMENT PROCESS

The Software Development Process is the structure approach to developing software for a system or project. There are a number of approaches that can be used to include waterfall, spiral and incremental development. These different approaches will focus the testing effort at different points in the development process. However, each is approach composed of the same basic steps of development.

Step 1: Planning

An important task in creating a software program is Requirements Analysis. Customers typically have an abstract idea of what they want as an end result, but not what software should do. Skilled and experienced software engineers recognize incomplete, ambiguous, or even contradictory requirements at this point. Frequently demonstrating live code may help reduce the risk that the requirements are incorrect. Once the general requirements are gathered from the client, an analysis of the scope of the development should be determined and clearly stated. This is often called a Statement of Objectives (SOO).

Step 2: Implementation

Implementation is the part of the process where software engineers actually program the code for the project.

Step 3: Testing

Software testing is an integral and important phase of the software development process. This part of the process ensures that defects are recognized as soon as possible. It can also provide an objective, independent view of the software to allow users to appreciate and understand the risks of software deployment. Software testing can be stated as the process of validating and verifying that a software program/application/product:

- Meets the requirements that guided its design and development;

- Works as expected; and

- Can be implemented with the same characteristics.

Step 4: Deployment and Maintenance

Deployment starts after the code is appropriately tested, approved for release, and sold or otherwise distributed into a production environment. This may involve installation, customization, testing, and possibly an extended period of evaluation. Software training and support is important, as software is only effective if it is used correctly. Maintaining and enhancing software to cope with newly discovered faults or requirements can take substantial time and effort, as missed requirements may force redesign of the software.

Software Development Process Models

A software development process model (SDPM) or software life-cycle model, is the process by which an organization develops software.

Major Software Development Models:

- The Waterfall Model

- Iterative and Incremental Models

- The Spiral Model

- The Rational Unified Process

- Agile Models

The Waterfall Model

- The best known process model. Dates from 1970 are though widely derided, it remains widely used and its terminology forms the basis for almost all discussions of other SDPMs.

- Defining characteristic: movement from phase to phase is always forward (downhill), irreversible. Milestones are set at each phase transition:

  ◦ Schedule deadlines,

  ◦ Required reports,

  ◦ Required approval to move on.

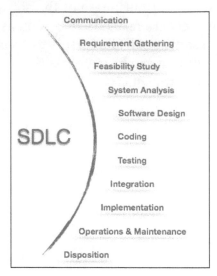

- The waterfall model gets its name from the fact that the first diagrams of this process illustrated it as a series of terraces over which a stream flowed, cascading down from one level to another. The point of this portrayal was that water always flows downhill — it can't reverse itself. Similarly, the defining characteristic of the waterfall model is the irreversible forward progress from phase to phase.

Waterfall is often criticized as inflexible, in large part because of that irreversible forward motion. Many organizations, in practice, will do a kind of "waterfall with appeals", allowing developers to revisit and revise decisions and documents from earlier phases after jumping through a number of deliberately restrictive hoops.

Verification and Validation

Verification & Validation: assuring that a software system meets the users' needs. The principle objectives are:

- The discovery of defects in a system.

- The assessment of whether or not the system is usable in an operational situation.

Difference between Verification and Validation

- Verification:

  ◦ "Are we building the product right" (Boehm).

  ◦ The software should conform to its (most recent) specification.

- Validation:
  - ◦ "Are we building the right product".
  - ◦ The software should do what the user really requires.

Verification is essentially looking for mistakes in our most recent bit of work by comparing what we have now to the most recent "official" document defining our system.

Validation is a return to first principles, comparing what we have now to what we (or our customers) originally wanted.

You might think that, in a process divided into steps, if we do each step "correctly", then the entire sequence must be "correct". In practice, though, the accumulation of small errors can lead to massive alterations over time.

Most V&V activities mix verification and validation together to different degrees.

Testing

- Testing is the act of executing a program with selected data to uncover bugs. As opposed to debugging, which is the process of finding the faulty code responsible for failed tests.

- Testing is the most common, but not the only form of V&V Industry faults per 100 statements is quite common.

Is testing verification or validation? A great deal depends on how we decide whether the test output is correct. If we do this by viewing the data ourselves and looking for things that jump out to our eyes as "wrong", then we are doing mainly validation. On the other hand, if part of our design process was to set up a set of tests with files of their expected outputs, and we are simply comparing the actual output files to the expected output files, then we are doing more verification.

Testing throughout the Waterfall

Testing Stages

- Unit Test: Tests of individual subroutines and modules,
  - ◦ Usually conducted by the programmer.
- Integration Test: Tests of "subtrees" of the total project hierarchy chart (groups of subroutines calling each other).
  - ◦ Generally a team responsibility.
- System Test: Test of the entire system,
  - ◦ Supervised by team leaders or by V&V specialists.
  - ◦ Many companies have independent teams for this purpose.
- Regression Test: Unit/Integration/System tests that are repeated after a change has been made to the code.

- Acceptance Test: A test conducted by the customers or their representatives to decide whether to purchase/accept a developed system.

Not Just in One Phase

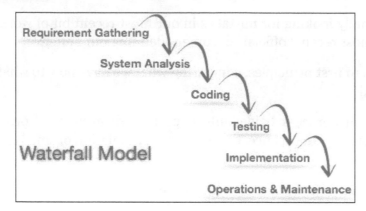

Although the waterfall model shows V&V as a separate phase near the end, we know that some forms of V&V occur much earlier.

- Requirements are validated in consultation with the customers.

- Unit testing occurs during Implementation, etc.

So this phase of the waterfall model really describes system and acceptance testing.

A Still-broader View

Even the "V&V" does not capture the full context of V&V:

- Requirements must be validated,

- Designs may be validated & verified,

- Maintenance changes are tested.

Advantages of Waterfall

- Linear structure is easy to understand,

- Development progress is easily estimated and explicitly documented,

- Widely known,

- Scales well.

Disadvantages of Waterfall

- Inflexible: corrections limited to current phase.

- In some projects, requirements are not known or understood early in the life-cycle.

- Working version of system is only available near the end.

- Often becomes a documentation mill.

Iterative/Incremental Development

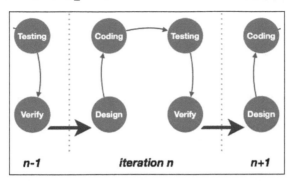

- A variety of related approaches a counter-reaction to what many believe to be an overly rigid, management-focused, waterfall model.

- Emphasize quick cycles of development, usually with earlier and more user-oriented validation.

- Requirements specification, design and implementation are interleaved.

- Each version adds a small amount of additional functionality.

As a counter-reaction to what many believe to be an overly rigid waterfall model, there are a variety of incremental approaches that emphasize quick cycles of development, usually with earlier and more user-oriented validation.

There is a greater emphasis on producing intermediate versions, each adding a small amount of additional functionality. Some of these are *releases*, either external (released outside the team) or internal (seen only by the team), which may have been planned earlier.

Difference between Iterative and Incremental

- "Iterative" means that we can re-visit decisions, design, and code produced in earlier iterative steps.

- "Incremental" means that each iteration produces just a small unit of additional functional behavior. We don't try to build major subsystems of the project in a single pass.

   ○ This often requires a more "vertical" view in which we implement a bit of high level control code and pieces of related low-level code.

   ○ As opposed to the "horizontal" approach of working "bottom up" and implementing the low-level ADTS, then the code that calls, upon them, then ending with the top-level interface to the whole program.

   ○ Or the "horizontal" approach of working "top down" and implementing the most abstract code (the GUI or command-line interfaces), then functions that they call, then the ending with the lowest-level ADTS that don't call on anything else.

Iterative versus Incremental Models

- Iterative: We do some set of process steps repeatedly. To use a programming analogy, this is iterative:

  while (!done) {

     ⋮

  }

- Incremental: We accumulate value in small steps. To use a programming analogy, this is incremental:

  total += x;

Incremental development is almost always iterative, but you can be iterative without being incremental.

Variations

- Some projects employ throw-away prototyping, versions whose code is only used to demonstrate and evaluate possibilities. This can lead to insight into poorly understood requirements.

- Evolutionary prototyping keeps the prototypes, gradually evolving them into the final deliverable.

- Some waterfall projects may employ incremental schemes for parts of large systems (e.g., the user interface).

Advantages

- Ability to explore poorly understood requirements,

- Flexibility,

- Working implementation is available early.

Disadvantages

- Poor process visibility (e.g., are we on schedule?).

- Continual small drifts from the main architecture leading to poorly structured systems.

- Dead-ends (the local optimization problem).

The Spiral Model

An iterative approach with a focus on risk management. Each iteration builds on the earlier ones risk: an uncertain outcome with a potential for loss.

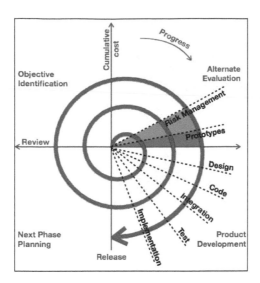

Examples:

- Team inexperience,

- Inability to meet schedule,

- Uncertainty in requirements.

Spiral Phases

- Determine objectives, alternatives and constraints:

  - Define requirements,

  - Alternatives (including, e.g., 3rd-party code) identified,

  - Constraints defined.

- Identify and resolve risks, evaluate alternatives:

  - Evaluate identified alternatives,

  - Identify risks,

  - Resolve risks,

  - Produce prototype.

- Develop and test:

  - Analyze performance of prototype,

  - Create & review design, code, test.

- Plan next iteration:

  - Often includes customer evaluation of prototype or current project iteration.

Advantages of Spiral Model

- Flexible – emphasis on alleviating risks as they are identified,

- Considerable opportunity for validation,

- Scales well,

- Good process visibility,

- Working releases/prototypes produced early.

Disadvantages of Spiral Model

- Can be costly (slow?),

- Risk analysis is a specialized skill, but critical to project success.

Rational Unified Process

- 1997, Jacobsen, Booch, and Rumbaugh.

- Best Practices:
  - Develop iteratively
  - Manage requirements
  - Use components
  - Model visually
  - Verify quality
  - Control changes

These three were already some of the biggest names in OOA&D before they decided to collaborate on a unified version of their previously distinctive approaches.

Their collaboration coincided with their being hired by Rational Corp., a major vendor of software development tools. Hence the "Rational" in RUP refers to the name of the company. It's not bragging. They aren't saying that this is a uniquely intellectual approach or that Waterfall, Spiral, et. al., are "irrational".

Unified Model Phases

- Inception: Initial concept-
  - Pitching the project concept,
  - Usually informal, low details,
  - "Perhaps we should build a".

- Elaboration: Exploring requirements-

    ◦ Adding detail to our understanding of what the system should do.

    ◦ Produces.

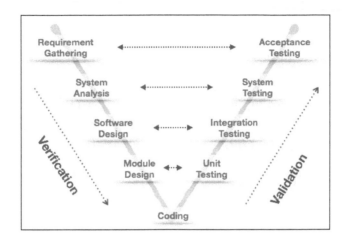

Unified Model Phases Continued

- Construction: Building the software-

    ◦ Design & implementation.

- Transition: Final packaging-

    ◦ Activities that can't be done incrementally during construction, e.g.,

    ◦ Performance tuning,

    ◦ User training.

Releases

One task during Elaboration is to plan releases:

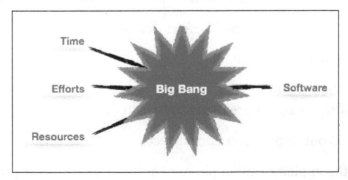

- Major phases are divided into increments, each of which ends with a release.

- A release is some kind of product that implements some part of the required functionality:

    ◦ Its existence and acceptance by management shows that we are ready to move on.

- The release plan records decisions about:

  ○ How many releases there will be,

  ○ What functionality will be added with each release,

  ○ When the releases will be made,

  ○ Which releases are internal (i.e., only the development team sees them) and which are external.

The term "increments" gets used a lot in different models. Sometimes it refers, as it does here, to the time period during which the next release of the software is developed. In other cases it refers to the next version of the software. In other cases it refers to the software release itself.

Key Concepts of the RUP

Common Workflows

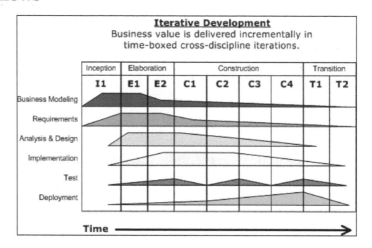

- Although waterfall and other SDPMs treat analysis, design, etc., as one-time phases.

- Careful study shows that developers do analysis, design, etc., *activities* continuously:

  ○ Analysis: what do we need the (currently considered part of the) system to do,

  ○ Design: how do we get it to do that,

  ○ Implementation: write out that series of design decisions in an appropriate notation (e.g., code, diagrams, requirements statements),

  ○ Validation: Is our implementation correct.

For example, deep in the implementation phase of a Waterfall project, a programmer is assigned a function to implement.

That programmer will:

- Think carefully about *what* the function is supposed to do (analysis).

- Choose an algorithm that will accomplish that (design).

- Code the function (implementation).

- Unit-test that function (validation).

But we aren't *in* the analysis, design, or validation *phases*. The diagram on the right is supposed to illustrate that, although the percentage of time devoted to the activities of analysis, design, implementation, and validation, none of those activites ever entirely go away and are, once and for all, *done*.

A process model may still use some of these same terms as the name for major phases, but that's really a different sense of the terms. For example, the "Design" phase of the Waterfall is when the language in which we "implement" is the collection of notations and diagrams that we use for system design. But we still analyze, design, implement, and validate our Design decisions.

ADIV

In the RUP, all progress is made as continual ADIV cycles. ADIV: Analysis, Design, Implementation, Validation.

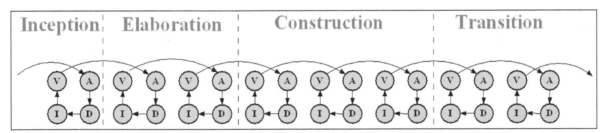

An Evolution of Models

RUP supports development via a series of models. The most important of these are:

- Domain Model

  ○ A model of the application domain as it currently exists, *before* we began our new development project.

  ○ Ensures that the development team understands the world that the system will work in.

- Analysis Model

  ○ A model of how the world will interact with the software system that we envision.

  ○ Expresses *what* the system will do when it is working.

- Design Model

  ○ Describes *how* we can get the system to do the things the analysis model says it should do.

Models Evolved

RUP embraces the Object-Oriented philosophy.

- Every program is a simulation.

- The quality of a program's design is proportional to how faithfully the objects and interactions in the program reflect those in the real world.

- Domain, analysis, and design models all focus on how classes of objects interact with one another.

- Most of the classes in the design are presumed to have already been described as part of the analysis model.

- Most of the classes in the analysis model are presumed to have already been described as part of the domain model.

Advantages of RUP

- Process details are expressed in general terms, allowing local customization.

- Heavy emphasis on documentation (UML).

- Can embrace incremental releases.

- Evolutionary approach can lead to clean implementations.

Disadvantages of RUP

- Process details are expressed in general terms, providing minimal guidance and requiring local customization,

- Complex,

- Heavy documentation can be expensive.

Agile Methods

A modern variant of incremental development. Agile development is:

- A reaction against heavily-managed, documentation-heavy processes.

- A social movement within the software development profession:

  ○ Introduced in the Agile Manifesto.

Emphasis Areas

Emphasis is on:

- Iterative & incremental development.

- Frequent communication with customer representatives:

  ◦ Work is organized via "user stories".

- Short "time-boxed" development cycles.

- Focus on quality as a matter of professional pride.

- Adoption of professional best-practices.

SOFTWARE REQUIREMENTS

Requirement is a condition or capability possessed by the software or system component in order to solve a real world problem. The problems can be to automate a part of a system, to correct shortcomings of an existing system, to control a device, and so on. IEEE defines requirement as condition or capability needed by a user to solve a problem or achieve an objective. A condition or capability that must be met or possessed by a system or system component to satisfy a contract, standard, specification, or other formally imposed documents. Requirements describe how a system should act, appear or perform. For this, when users request for software, they provide an approximation of what the new system should be capable of doing. Requirements differ from one user to another and from one business process to another.

Guidelines for Expressing Requirements

The purpose of the requirements document is to provide a basis for the mutual understanding between the users and the designers of the initial definition of the software development life cycle (SDLC) including the requirements, operating environment and development plan.

The requirements document should include the overview, the proposed methods and procedures, a summary of improvements, a summary of impacts, security, privacy, internal control considerations, cost considerations, and alternatives. The requirements section should state the functions required in the software in quantitative and qualitative terms and how these functions will satisfy the performance objectives. The requirements document should also specify the performance requirements such as accuracy, validation, timing, and flexibility. Inputs, outputs, and data characteristics need to be explained. Finally, the requirements document needs to describe the operating environment and provide (or make reference to) a development plan.

There is no standard method to express and document requirements. Requirements can be stated efficiently by the experience of knowledgeable individuals, observing past requirements, and by following guidelines. Guidelines act as an efficient method of expressing requirements, which also provide a basis for software development, system testing, and user satisfaction. The guidelines that are commonly followed to document requirements are listed below:

1. Sentences and paragraphs should be short and written in active voice. Also, proper grammar, spelling, and punctuation should be used.

2. Conjunctions such as 'and' and 'or' should be avoided as they indicate the combination of several requirements in one requirement.

3. Each requirement should be stated only once so that it does not create redundancy in the requirements specification document.

Types of Requirements

Requirements help to understand the behavior of a system, which is described by various tasks of the system. For example, some of the tasks of a system are to provide a response to input values, determine the state of data objects, and so on. Note that requirements are considered prior to the development of the software. The requirements, which are commonly considered, are classified into three categories, namely, functional requirements, non-functional requirements, and domain requirements.

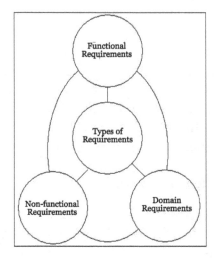

IEEE defines functional requirements as 'a function that a system or component must be able to perform.' These requirements describe the interaction of software with its environment and specify the inputs, outputs, external interfaces, and the functions that should be included in the software. Also, the services provided by functional requirements specify the procedure by which the software should react to particular inputs or behave in particular situations.

To understand functional requirements properly, let us consider the following example of an on-line banking system:

1. The user of the bank should be able to search the desired services from the available ones.

2. There should be appropriate documents' for users to read. This implies that when a user wants to open an account in the bank, the forms must be available so that the user can open an account.

3. After registration, the user should be provided with a unique acknowledgement number so that he can later be given an account number.

The functional requirements describe the specific services provided by the online banking system. These requirements indicate user requirements and specify that functional requirements may be described at different levels of detail in an online banking system. With the help of these functional requirements, users can easily view, search and download registration forms and other information about the bank. On the other hand, if requirements are not stated properly, they are misinterpreted by software engineers and user requirements are not met.

The functional requirements should be complete and consistent. Completeness implies that all the user requirements are defined. Consistency implies that all requirements are specified clearly without any contradictory definition. Generally, it is observed that completeness and consistency cannot be achieved in large software or in a complex system due to the problems that arise while defining the functional requirements of these systems. The different needs of stakeholders also prevent the achievement of completeness and consistency. Due to these reasons, requirements may not be obvious when they are, 'first specified and may further lead to inconsistencies in the requirements specification.

The non-functional requirements (also known as quality requirements) are related to system attributes such as reliability and response time. Non-functional requirements arise due to user requirements, budget constraints, organizational policies, and so on. These requirements are not related directly to any particular function provided by the system.

Non-functional requirements should be accomplished in software to make it perform efficiently. For example, if an aero plane is unable to fulfill reliability requirements, it is not approved for safe operation. Similarly, if a real time control system is ineffective in accomplishing non-functional requirements, the control functions cannot operate correctly.

The description of different types of non-functional requirements is listed below:

1. Product requirements: These requirements specify how software product performs.

2. Efficiency requirements: Describe the extent to which the software makes optimal use of resources, the speed with which the system executes, and the memory it consumes for its operation. For example, the system should be able to operate at least three times faster than the existing system.

3. Reliability requirements: Describe the acceptable failure rate of the software. For example, the software should be able to operate even if a hazard occurs.

4. Portability requirements: Describe the ease with which the software can be transferred from one platform to another. For example, it should be easy to port the software to a different operating system without the need to redesign the entire software.

5. Usability requirements: Describe the ease with which users are able to operate the software. For example, the software should be able to provide access to functionality with fewer keystrokes and mouse clicks.

6. Organizational requirements: These requirements are derived from the policies and procedures of an organization.

7. Delivery requirements: Specify when the software and its documentation are to be delivered to the user.

8. Implementation requirements: Describe requirements such as programming language and design method.

9. Standards requirements: Describe the process standards to be used during software development. For example, the software should be developed using standards specified by the ISO and IEEE standards.

10. External requirements: These requirements include all the requirements that affect the software or its development process externally. External requirements comprise the following.

11. Interoperability requirements: Define the way in which different computer based systems will interact with each other in one or more organizations.

12. Ethical requirements: Specify the rules and regulations of the software so that they are acceptable to users.

13. Legislative requirements: Ensure that the software operates within the legal jurisdiction. For example, pirated software should not be sold.

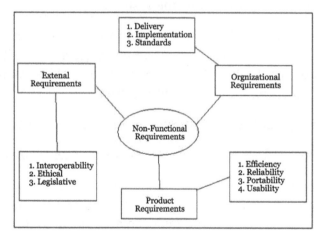

Non-functional requirements are difficult to verify. Hence, it is essential to write non-functional requirements quantitatively, so that they can be tested. For this, non-functional requirements metrics are used.

Metrics for Non-functional Requirements

Features	Measures
Speed	• Processed transaction/ second • User/event response time • Screen refresh rate
Size	• Amount of memory (KB) • Number of RAM chips.
Ease of use	• Training time • Number of help windows

Reliability	• Mean time to failure (MTTF)
	• Portability of unavailability
	• Rate of failure occurrence
Robustness	• Time to restart after failure
	• Percentage of events causing failure
	• Probability of data corruption on failure
Portability	• Percentage of target-dependent statements
	• Number of target systems

Requirements which are derived from the application domain of the system instead from the needs of the users are known as domain requirements. These requirements may be new functional requirements or specify a method to perform some particular computations. In addition, these requirements include any constraint that may be present in the existing functional requirements. As domain requirements reflect the fundamentals of the application domain, it is important to understand these requirements. Also, if these requirements are not fulfilled, it may be difficult to make .the system work as desired.

A system can include a number of domain requirements. For example, it may comprise a design constraint that describes the user interface, which is capable of accessing all the databases used in a system. It is important for a development team to create databases and interface designs as per established standards. Similarly, the requirements of the user such as copyright restrictions and security mechanism for the files and documents used in the system are also domain requirements. When domain requirements are not expressed clearly, it can result in the following difficulties.

- Problem of understandability: When domain requirements are specified in the language of application domain (such as mathematical expressions), it becomes difficult for software engineers to understand them.

- Problem of implicitness: When domain experts understand the domain requirements but do not express these requirements clearly, it may create a problem (due to incomplete information) for the development team to understand and implement the requirements in the system.

Requirements Engineering Process

This process is a series of activities that are performed in the requirements phase to express requirements in the Software Requirements Specification (SRS) document. It focuses on understanding the requirements and its type so that an appropriate technique is determined to carry out the Requirements Engineering (RE) process. The new software developed after collecting requirements either replaces the existing software or enhances its features and functionality. For example, the payment mode of the existing software can be changed from payment through hand-written cheques to electronic payment of bills.

An RE process is shown, which comprises various steps including feasibility study, requirements elicitation, requirements analysis, requirements specification, requirements validation, and requirements management.

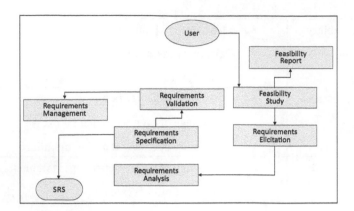

The requirements engineering process begins with feasibility study of the requirements. Then requirements elicitation is performed, which focuses on gathering user requirements. After the requirements are gathered, an analysis is performed, which further leads to requirements specification. The output of this is stored in the form of software requirements specification document. Next, the requirements are checked for their completeness and correctness in requirements validation. Last of all, to understand and control changes to system requirements, requirements management is performed.

SOFTWARE DESIGN

Once the requirements document for the software to be developed is available, the software design phase begins. While the requirement specification activity deals entirely with the problem domain, design is the first phase of transforming the problem into a solution. In the design phase, the customer and business requirements and technical considerations all come together to formulate a product or a system.

The design process comprises a set of principles, concepts and practices, which allow a software engineer to model the system or product that is to be built. This model, known as design model, is assessed for quality and reviewed before a code is generated and tests are conducted. The design model provides details about software data structures, architecture, interfaces and components which are required to implement the system.

Basic of Software Design

Software design is a phase in software engineering, in which a blueprint is developed to serve as a base for constructing the software system. IEEE defines software design as 'both process of defining, the architecture, components, interfaces, and other characteristics of a system or component and the result of that process.' In the design phase, many critical and strategic decisions are made to achieve the desired functionality and quality of the system. These decisions are taken into account to successfully develop the software and carry out its maintenance in a way that the quality of the end product is improved.

Principles of Software Design

Developing design is a cumbersome process as most expansive errors are often introduced in this phase. Moreover, if these errors get unnoticed till later phases, it becomes more difficult to correct them. Therefore, a number of principles are followed while designing the software. These principles act as a framework for the designers to follow a good design practice.

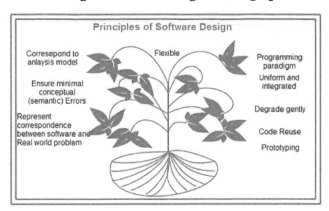

Some of the commonly followed design principles are as following:

1. Software design should correspond to the analysis model: Often a design element corresponds to many requirements, therefore, we must know how the design model satisfies all the requirements represented by the analysis model.

2. Choose the right programming paradigm: A programming paradigm describes the structure of the software system. Depending on the nature and type of application, different programming paradigms such as procedure oriented, object-oriented, and prototyping paradigms can be used. The paradigm should be chosen keeping constraints in mind such as time, availability of resources and nature of user's requirements.

3. Software design should be uniform and integrated: Software design is considered uniform and integrated, if the interfaces are properly defined among the design components. For this, rules, format, and styles are established before the design team starts designing the software.

4. Software design should be flexible: Software design should be flexible enough to adapt changes easily. To achieve the flexibility, the basic design concepts such as abstraction, refinement, and modularity should be applied effectively.

5. Software design should ensure minimal conceptual (semantic) errors: The design team must ensure that major conceptual errors of design such as ambiguousness and inconsistency are addressed in advance before dealing with the syntactical errors present in the design model.

6. Software design should be structured to degrade gently: Software should be designed to handle unusual changes and circumstances, and if the need arises for termination, it must do so in a proper manner so that functionality of the software is not affected.

7. Software design should represent correspondence between the software and real-world problem: The software design should be structured in such away that it always relates with the real-world problem.

8. Software reuse: Software engineers believe on the phrase: 'do not reinvent the wheel'. Therefore, software components should be designed in such a way that they can be effectively reused to increase the productivity.

9. Designing for testability: A common practice that has been followed is to keep the testing phase separate from the design and implementation phases. That is, first the software is developed (designed and implemented) and then handed over to the testers who subsequently determine whether the software is fit for distribution and subsequent use by the customer. However, it has become apparent that the process of separating testing is seriously flawed, as if any type of design or implementation errors are found after implementation, then the entire or a substantial part of the software requires to be redone. Thus, the test engineers should be involved from the initial stages. For example, they should be involved with analysts to prepare tests for determining whether the user requirements are being met.

10. Prototyping: Prototyping should be used when the requirements are not completely defined in the beginning. The user interacts with the developer to expand and refine the requirements as the development proceeds. Using prototyping, a quick 'mock-up' of the system can be developed. This mock-up can be used as a effective means to give the users a feel of what the system will look like and demonstrate functions that will be included in the developed system. Prototyping also helps in reducing risks of designing software that is not in accordance with the customer's requirements.

The design principles are often constrained by the existing hardware configuration, the implementation language, the existing file and data structures, and the existing organizational practices. Also, the evolution of each software design should be meticulously designed for future evaluations, references and maintenance.

Software Design Concepts

Every software process is characterized by basic concepts along with certain practices or methods. Methods represent the manner through which the concepts are applied. As new technology replaces older technology, many changes occur in the methods that are used to apply the concepts for the development of software. However, the fundamental concepts underlining the software design process remain the same.

Abstraction

Abstraction refers to a powerful design tool, which allows software designers to consider components at an abstract level, while neglecting the implementation details of the components. IEEE defines abstraction as 'a view of a problem that extracts the essential information relevant to a particular purpose and ignores the remainder of the information'. The concept of abstraction can be used in two ways: as a process and as an entity. As a process, it refers to a mechanism of hiding irrelevant details and representing only the essential features of an item so that one can focus on important things at a time. As an entity, it refers to a model or view of an item.

Each step in the software process is accomplished through various levels of abstraction. At the highest level, an outline of the solution to the problem is presented whereas at the lower levels, the solution to the problem is presented in detail. For example, in the requirements analysis phase, a solution to the problem is presented using the language of problem environment and as we proceed through the software process, the abstraction level reduces and at the lowest level, source code of the software is produced.

There are three commonly used abstraction mechanisms in software design, namely, functional abstraction, data abstraction and control abstraction. All these mechanisms allow us to control the complexity of the design process by proceeding from the abstract design model to concrete design model in a systematic manner.

1. Functional abstraction: This involves the use of parameterized subprograms. Functional abstraction can be generalized as collections of subprograms referred to as 'groups'. Within these groups there exist routines which may be visible or hidden. Visible routines can be used within the containing groups as well as within other groups, whereas hidden routines are hidden from other groups and can be used within the containing group only.

2. Data abstraction: This involves specifying data that describes a data object. For example, the data object *window* encompasses a set of attributes (window type, window dimension) that describe the window object clearly. In this abstraction mechanism, representation and manipulation details are ignored.

3. Control abstraction: This states the desired effect, without stating the exact mechanism of control. For example, if and while statements in programming languages (like C and C++) are abstractions of machine code implementations, which involve conditional instructions. In the architectural design level, this abstraction mechanism permits specifications of sequential subprogram and exception handlers without the concern for exact details of implementation.

Architecture

Software architecture refers to the structure of the system, which is composed of various components of a program/system, the attributes (properties) of those components and the relationship amongst them. The software architecture enables the software engineers to analyze the software design efficiently. In addition, it also helps them in decision-making and handling risks. The software architecture does the following:

*   Provides an insight to all the interested stakeholders that enable them to communicate with each other.

*   Highlights early design decisions, which have great impact on the software engineering activities (like coding and testing) that follow the design phase.

*   Creates intellectual models of how the system is organized into components and how these components interact with each other.

Currently, software architecture is represented in an informal and unplanned manner. Though the architectural concepts are often represented in the infrastructure (for supporting particular architectural styles) and the initial stages of a system configuration, the lack of an explicit independent characterization of architecture restricts the advantages of this design concept in the present scenario.

Note that software architecture comprises two elements of design model, namely, data design and architectural design.

Patterns

A pattern provides a description of the solution to a recurring design problem of some specific domain in such a way that the solution can be used again and again. The objective of each pattern is to provide an insight to a designer who can determine the following:

1. Whether the pattern can be reused;

2. Whether the pattern is applicable to the current project;

3. Whether the pattern can be used to develop a similar but functionally or structurally different design pattern.

Types of Design Patterns

Software engineer can use the design pattern during the entire software design process. When the analysis model is developed, the designer can examine the problem description at different levels of abstraction to determine whether it complies with one or more of the following types of design patterns.

1. Architectural patterns: These patterns are high-level strategies that refer to the overall structure and organization of a software system. That is, they define the elements of a software system such as subsystems, components, classes, etc. In addition, they also indicate the relationship between the elements along with the rules and guidelines for specifying these relationships. Note that architectural patterns are often considered equivalent to software architecture.

2. Design patterns: These patterns are medium-level strategies that are used to solve design problems. They provide a means for the refinement of the elements (as defined by architectural pattern) of a software system or the relationship among them. Specific design elements such as relationship among components or mechanisms that affect component-to-component interaction are addressed by design patterns. Note that design patterns are often considered equivalent to software components.

3. Idioms: These patterns are low-level patterns, which are programming-language specific. They describe the implementation of a software component, the method used for interaction among software components, etc., in a specific programming language. Note that idioms are often termed as coding patterns.

Modularity

Modularity is achieved by dividing the software into uniquely named and addressable components, which are also known as modules. A complex system (large program) is partitioned into a set of discrete modules in such a way that each module can be developed independent of other modules. After developing the modules, they are integrated together to meet the software requirements. Note that larger the number of modules a system is divided into, greater will be the effort required to integrate the modules.

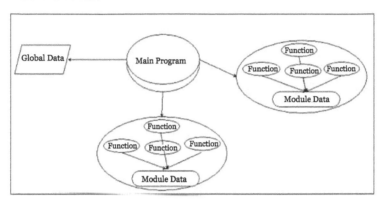

Modularizing a design helps to plan the development in a more effective manner, accommodate changes easily, conduct testing and debugging effectively and efficiently, and conducts maintenance work without adversely affecting the functioning of the software.

Information Hiding

Modules should be specified and designed in such a way that the data structures and processing details of one module are not accessible to other modules. They pass only that much information to each other, which is required to accomplish the software functions. The way of hiding unnecessary details is referred to as information hiding. IEEE defines information hiding as 'the technique of encapsulating software design decisions in modules in such a way that the module's interfaces reveal as little as possible about the module's inner workings; thus each module is a 'black box' to the other modules in the system.

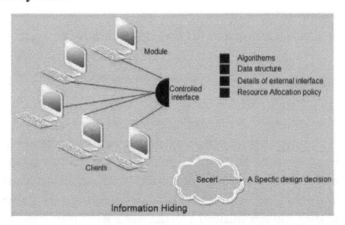

Information hiding is of immense use when modifications are required during the testing and maintenance phase. Some of the advantages associated with information hiding are listed below:

1. Leads to low coupling.

2. Emphasizes communication through controlled interfaces.

3. Decreases the probability of adverse effects.

4. Restricts the effects of changes in one component on others.

5. Results in higher quality software.

Stepwise Refinement

Stepwise refinement is a top-down design strategy used for decomposing a system from a high level of abstraction into a more detailed level (lower level) of abstraction. At the highest level of abstraction, function or information is defined conceptually without providing any information about the internal workings of the function or internal structure of the data. As we proceed towards the lower levels of abstraction, more and more details are available.

Software designers start the stepwise refinement process by creating a sequence of compositions for the system being designed. Each composition is more detailed than the previous one and contains more components and interactions. The earlier compositions represent the significant interactions within the system, while the later compositions show in detail how these interactions are achieved.

To have a clear understanding of the concept, let us consider an example of stepwise refinement. Every computer program comprises input, process, and output.

- Input

  o Get user's name (string) through a prompt.

  o Get user's grade (integer from 0 to 100) through a prompt and validate.

- Process

- Output

Stepwise refinement can also be performed for process and output phase.

Refactoring

Refactoring is an important design activity that reduces the complexity of module design keeping its behaviour or function unchanged. Refactoring can be defined as a process of modifying a software system to improve the internal structure of design without changing its external behavior. During the refactoring process, the existing design is checked for any type of flaws like redundancy, poorly constructed algorithms and data structures, etc., in order to improve the design. For example, a design model might yield a component which exhibits low cohesion (like a component performs four functions that have a limited relationship with one another). Software designers may decide to refactor the component into four different components, each exhibiting high cohesion. This leads to easier integration, testing, and maintenance of the software components.

Structural Partitioning

When the architectural style of a design follows a hierarchical nature, the structure of the program can be partitioned either horizontally or vertically. In horizontal partitioning, the control modules are used to communicate between functions and execute the functions. Structural partitioning provides the following benefits.

- The testing and maintenance of software becomes easier.

- The negative impacts spread slowly.

- The software can be extended easily.

Besides these advantages, horizontal partitioning has some disadvantage also. It requires to pass more data across the module interface, which makes the control flow of the problem more complex. This usually happens in cases where data moves rapidly from one function to another.

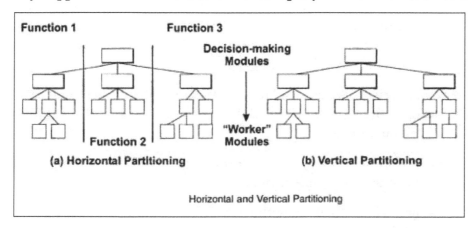

Horizontal and Vertical Partitioning

In vertical partitioning, the functionality is distributed among the modules--in a top-down manner. The modules at the top level called control modules perform the decision-making and do little processing whereas the modules at the low level called worker modules perform all input, computation and output tasks.

Concurrency

Computer has limited resources and they must be utilized efficiently as much as possible. To utilize these resources efficiently, multiple tasks must be executed concurrently. This requirement makes concurrency one of the major concepts of software design. Every system must be designed to allow multiple processes to execute concurrently, whenever possible. For example, if the current process is waiting for some event to occur, the system must execute some other process in the mean time.

However, concurrent execution of multiple processes sometimes may result in undesirable situations such as an inconsistent state, deadlock, etc. For example, consider two processes A and B and a data item Q1 with the value '200'. Further, suppose A and B are being executed concurrently and firstly A reads the value of Q1 (which is '200') to add '100' to it. However, before A updates es the value of Q1, B reads the value ofQ1 (which is still '200') to add '50' to it. In this situation, whether A or B first updates the value of Q1, the value of would definitely be wrong resulting in an inconsistent state of the system. This is because the actions of A and B are not synchronized with each other. Thus, the system must control the concurrent execution and synchronize the actions of concurrent processes.

One way to achieve synchronization is mutual exclusion, which ensures that two concurrent processes do not interfere with the actions of each other. To ensure this, mutual exclusion may use locking technique. In this technique, the processes need to lock the data item to be read or updated. The data item locked by some process cannot be accessed by other processes until it is unlocked. It implies that the process, that needs to access the data item locked by some other process, has to wait.

Developing a Design Model

To develop a complete specification of design (design model), four design models are needed. These models are listed below:

1. Data design: This specifies the data structures for implementing the software by converting data objects and their relationships identified during the analysis phase. Various studies suggest that design engineering should begin with data design, since this design lays the foundation for all other design models.

2. Architectural design: This specifies the relationship between the structural elements of the software, design patterns, architectural styles, and the factors affecting the ways in which architecture can be implemented.

3. Component-level design: This provides the detailed description of how structural elements of software will actually be implemented.

4. Interface design: This depicts how the software communicates with the system that interoperates with it and with the end-users.

ASPECT-ORIENTED SOFTWARE DEVELOPMENT

In computing, aspect-oriented software development (AOSD) is a software development technology that seeks new modularizations of software systems in order to isolate secondary or supporting functions from the main program's business logic. AOSD allows multiple concerns to be expressed separately and automatically unified into working systems.

Traditional software development focuses on decomposing systems into units of primary functionality, while recognizing that there are other issues of concern that do not fit well into the primary decomposition. The traditional development process leaves it to the programmers to code modules corresponding to the primary functionality and to make sure that all other issues of concern are addressed in the code wherever appropriate. Programmers need to keep in mind all the things that need to be done, how to deal with each issue, the problems associated with the possible interactions, and the execution of the right behavior at the right time. These concerns span multiple primary functional units within the application, and often result in serious problems faced during application development and maintenance. The distribution of the code for realizing a concern becomes especially critical as the requirements for that concern evolve – a system maintainer must find and correctly update a variety of situations.

Aspect-oriented software development focuses on the identification, specification and representation of cross-cutting concerns and their modularization into separate functional units as well as their automated composition into a working system.

Motivation

Crosscutting Concerns

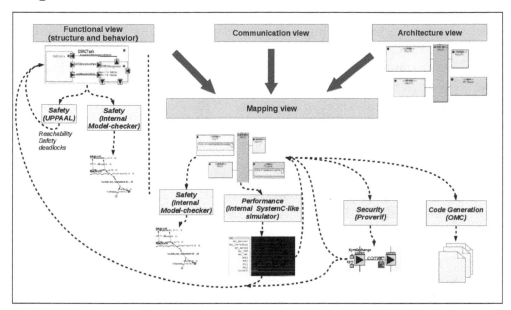

The motivation for aspect-oriented programming approaches stem from the problems caused by code scattering and tangling. The purpose of Aspect-Oriented Software Development is to provide systematic means to modularize crosscutting concerns.

The implementation of a concern is scattered if its code is spread out over multiple modules. The concern affects the implementation of multiple modules. Its implementation is not modular. The implementation of a concern is tangled if its code is intermixed with code that implements other concerns. The module in which tangling occurs is not cohesive.

Scattering and tangling often go together, even though they are different concepts. Aspect-oriented software development considers that code scattering and tangling are the symptoms of crosscutting concerns. Crosscutting concerns cannot be modularized using the decomposition mechanisms of the language (object or procedures) because they inherently follow different decomposition rules. The implementation and integration of these concerns with the primary functional decomposition of the system causes code tangling and scattering.

Examples:

1. Logging in Apache Tomcat: Classloading in Tomcat is a modular concern with respect to the system decomposition. Its implementation is contained in a small number of classes and is not intertwined with the implementation of other concerns. Logging in Tomcat is a crosscutting concern. Its implementation spreads over many classes and packages and is intermixed with the implementation of many other concerns.

2. Coordination of components: Figure represents the UML architecture diagram of a telecom component. Each box corresponds to a process that communicates with other processes through connectors.

Problems caused by Scattering and Tangling

Scattering and tangling of behavior are the symptoms that the implementation of a concern is not well modularized. A concern that is not modularized does not exhibit a well-defined interface. The interactions between the implementation of the concern and the modules of the system are not explicitly declared. They are encoded implicitly through the dependencies and interactions between fragments of code that implement the concern and the implementation of other modules. The lack of interfaces between the implementation of crosscutting concerns and the implementation of the modules of the system impedes the development, the evolution and the maintenance of the system.

System Development

A module is primarily a unit of independent development. It can be implemented to a large extent independently of other modules. Modularity is achieved through the definition of well-defined interfaces between segments of the system.

The lack of explicit interfaces between crosscutting concerns and the modules obtained through the functional decomposition of the system imply that the implementation of these concerns, as well as the responsibility with respect to the correct implementation of these concerns, cannot be assigned to independent development teams. This responsibility has to be shared among different developers that work on the implementation of different modules of the system and have to integrate the crosscutting concern with the module behavior.

Furthermore, modules whose implementation is tangled with crosscutting concerns are hard to reuse in different contexts. Crosscutting impedes reuse of components. The lack of interfaces between crosscutting concerns and other modules makes it hard to represent and reason about the overall architecture of a system. As the concern is not modularized, the interactions between the concern and the top-level components of the system are hard to represent explicitly. Hence, these concerns become hard to reason about because the dependencies between crosscutting concerns and components are not specified.

Finally, concerns that are not modularized are hard to test in isolation. The dependencies of the concern with respect to behavior of other modules are not declared explicitly. Hence, the implementation of unit test for such concerns requires knowledge about the implementation of many modules in the system.

System Maintenance and Evolution

The lack of support for the modular implementation of crosscutting concerns is especially problematic when the implementation of this concern needs to be modified. The comprehension of the implementation of a crosscutting concern requires the inspection of the implementation of all the modules with which it interacts. Hence, modifications of the system that affect the implementation of crosscutting concern require a manual inspection of all the locations in the code that are relevant to the crosscutting concern. The system maintainer must find and correctly update a variety of poorly identified situations.

Nature of Aspect-orientation

The focus of aspect-oriented software development is in the investigation and implementation of new structures for software modularity that provide support for explicit abstractions to modularize concerns. Aspect-oriented programming approaches provide explicit abstractions for the modular implementation of concerns in design, code, documentation, or other artifacts developed during the software life-cycle. These modularized concerns are called aspects, and aspect-oriented approaches provide methods to compose them. Some approaches denote a root concern as the base. Various approaches provide different flexibility with respect to composition of aspects.

Quantification and Obliviousness

The best known definition of the nature of AOSD is due to Filman and Friedman, which characterized AOSD using the equation *aspect orientation = quantification + obliviousness.*

AOP can be understood as the desire to make quantified statements about the behavior of programs, and to have these quantifications hold over programs written by oblivious programmers. AOP is the desire to make statements of the form: In program P, whenever condition C arises, perform action A over a conventionally coded program P.

Obliviousness implies that a program has no knowledge of which aspects modify it where or when, whereas quantification refers to the ability of aspects to affect multiple points in the program. The notion of non-invasiveness is often preferred to the term obliviousness. Non-invasiveness expresses that aspects can add behavior to a program without having to perform changes in that program, yet it does not assume that programs are not aware of the aspects.

Filman's definition of aspect-orientation is often considered too restrictive. Many aspect-oriented approaches use annotations to explicitly declare the locations in the system where aspects introduce behavior. These approaches require the manual inspection and modification of other modules in the system and are therefore invasive. Furthermore, aspect-orientation does not necessarily require quantification. Aspects can be used to isolate features whose implementation would otherwise be tangled with other features. Such aspects do not necessarily use quantification over multiple locations in the system.

The essential features of Aspect-Oriented Software Development are therefore better characterized in terms of the modularity of the implementation of crosscutting concerns, the abstractions provided by aspect-oriented languages to enable modularization and the expressiveness of the aspect-oriented composition operators.

Concepts and Terminology

Aspect-oriented approaches provide explicit support for localizing concerns into separated modules, called aspects. An aspect is a module that encapsulates a concern. Most aspect-oriented languages support the non-invasive introduction of behavior into a code base and quantification over points in the program where this behavior should be introduced. These points are called join points.

Join Point Model

Join points are points in the execution of the system, such as method calls, where behavior supplied by aspects is combined. A join point is a point in the execution of the program, which is used to define the dynamic structure of a crosscutting concern.

The join point model of an aspect-oriented language defines the types of join points that are supported by the aspect-oriented language and the possible interaction points between aspects and base modules.

The dynamic interpretation of join points makes it possible to expose runtime information such as the caller or callee of a method from a join point to a matching pointcut. Nowadays, there are various join point models around and still more under development. They heavily depend on the underlying programming language and AO language.

Examples of join points are:

- Method execution
- Method call
- Field read and write access
- Exception handler execution
- Static and dynamic initialization

A method call join point covers the actions of an object receiving a method call. It includes all the actions that compose a method call, starting after all arguments are evaluated up to return. Many AOP approaches implement aspect behavior by weaving hooks into join point shadows, which is the static projection of a join point onto the program code.

The highlighted join points include the execution of method moveBy(int, int) on a Line object, the calls to methods moveBy(int, int) on the Point objects in the context of the Line object, the execution of these methods in the context of the Point objects and the calls and execution of the setX(int) and setY(int) methods.

Pointcut Designators

The quantification over join points is expressed at the language level. This quantification may be implicit in the language structure or may be expressed using a query-like construct called a pointcut. Pointcuts are defined as a predicate over the syntax-tree of the program, and define an interface that constrains which elements of the base program are exposed by the pointcut. A pointcut picks out certain join points and values at those points. The syntactic formulation of a pointcut varies from approach to approach, but a pointcut can often be composed out of other pointcuts using the boolean operators AND, OR and NOT. Pointcut expressions can concisely capture a wide range of events of interests, using wildcards. For example, in AspectJ syntax, the move pointcut

```
pointcut move: call(public * Figure.* (..))
```

Picks out each call to Figure's public methods. flow poincuts identify join points based on whether they occur in the dynamic context of other join points. For example, in Aspect J syntax cflow(move()) picks out each join point that occurs in the dynamic context of the join points picked out by the move pointcut.

Pointcuts can be classified in two categories:

- Kinded pointcuts, such as the call pointcut, match one kind of join point using a signature.

- Non-kinded pointcuts, such as the cflow pointcut match all kinds of join points using a variety of properties.

Advice Bodies

An advice body is code that is executed when a join point is reached. Advice modularizes the functional details of a concern. The order in which the advice bodies contributed by aspects (and by the base) may be controlled in a variety of ways, including:

- As a join point is reached, before the execution proceeds with the base.

- After the base semantics for the join point. When the join point corresponds to the execution of a method, an after advice can be executed after the method returned or after raising an exception.

- As the join point is reached, with explicit control over whether the base semantics is executed. Around advice can modify the control flow of the program.

More general ways to describe the ordering of advice bodies in terms of partial-order graphs have also been provided. When the execution of a join point satisfies a pointcut expression, the base and advice code associated with the join point are executed. The advice may interact with the rest system through a join point instance containing reflective information on the context of the event that triggered the advice, such as the arguments of a method call or the target instance of a call.

Inter-type Declarations

Inter-type declarations allow the programmer to modify a program's static structure, such as class members and classes hierarchy. New members can be inserted and classes can be pushed down the class hierarchy.

Aspects

An aspect is a module that encapsulates a concern. An aspect is composed of pointcuts, advice bodies and inter-type declarations. In some approaches, an aspect may also contain classes and methods.

Aspect Weaving

Aspect weaving is a composition mechanism that coordinates aspects with the other modules of the system. It is performed by a specialized compiler, called an aspect weaver.

Example:

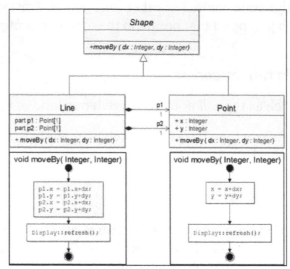

Editor in UML

Figure illustrates a classic example of a crosscutting concern in a figure editor example taken from the AOSD literature. The example describes an abstract Shape class that can be moved in the editor. Whenever a shape is moved, the display needs to be refreshed. Figure also depicts two Shape subclasses, Line and Point that implement the Shape functionality. The display refresh concern is scattered across the implementation of both subclasses. Figure represents an aspect-oriented implementation of the same system, where an aspect encapsulates the display updating functionality.

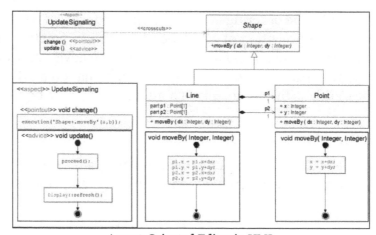

Aspect-Oriented Editor in UML

The move pointcut descriptor of figure captures all the executions of the move. By methods of a subclass of Shape and invokes the display refresh functionality after the execution proceeds. The concern is modularized, which makes it easier to evolve and maintain.

Aspect-oriented Requirement Engineering

Aspect-oriented requirement engineering (also referred to as "Early Aspects") focuses on the identification, specification and representation of crosscutting properties at the requirement level. Examples of such properties include security, mobility, availability and real-time constraints. Crosscutting properties are requirements, use cases or features that have a broadly scoped effect on other requirements or architecture components.

Aspect-oriented requirements engineering approaches are techniques that explicitly recognise the importance of clearly addressing both functional and non-functional crosscutting concerns in addition to non-crosscutting ones. Therefore, these approaches focus on systematically and modularly treating, reasoning about, composing and subsequently tracing crosscutting functional and non-functional concerns via suitable abstraction, representation and composition mechanisms tailored to the requirements engineering domain.

Specific areas of excellence under the denominator of AO Requirements Analysis are:

- The aspect-oriented requirements process itself,

- The aspect-oriented requirements notations,

- Aspect-oriented requirements tool support,

- Adoption and integration of aspect-oriented requirements engineering, and

- Assessment/evaluation of aspect-oriented requirements.

Aspect Oriented Business Process Management (AOBPM)

Reducing complexity is an important issue in Business Process Management (BPM) area. One source of complexity is rooted in the variety of concerns that a business process addresses, such as security and privacy. Ideally, these concerns should be defined separately from the business processes, as they typically span several processes, and they can be subject for change on a general organisational level instead of specific process level. However, current Business Process Management Systems do not support this kind of modelling. Aspect oriented business process management (AOBPM) tries to support separation of cross-cutting concerns from the core business concerns. It defines a set of requirements and a formal model. This model is designed using Coloured Petri Nets (CPN).

The approach is implemented as a service in YAWL based on Service Oriented Architecture.

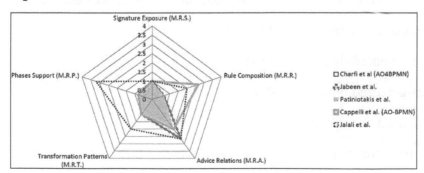

The assessment result of current aspect oriented business process management approaches are defined based on five dimensions such as Signature Exposure, Rule Composition, Advice Relations, Transformation Patterns, and Phases Support.

Aspect-oriented System Architecture

Aspect-oriented system architecture focuses on the localization and specification of crosscutting concerns in architectural designs. Crosscutting concerns that appear at the architectural level cannot be modularized by redefining the software architecture using conventional architectural abstractions. Aspect-oriented system architecture languages propose explicit mechanisms to identify, specify and evaluate aspects at the architecture design level.

Aspect-oriented architecture starts from the observation that we need to identify, specify and evaluate aspects explicitly at the architecture design level. Aspectual architecture approaches describe steps for identifying architectural aspects. This information is used to redesign a given architecture in which the architectural aspects are made explicit. In this regard, specific areas of excellence are:

- The aspect-oriented architecture process itself,

- The aspect-oriented architecture notations,

- Aspect-oriented architecture tool support,

- Adoption and integration of aspect-oriented architecture, and

- Assessment/evaluation of aspect-oriented architecture.

Aspect-oriented Modeling and Design

Aspect-oriented design has the same objectives as any software design activity, i.e. characterizing and specifying the behavior and structure of the software system. Its unique contribution to software design lies in the fact that concerns that are necessarily scattered and tangled in more traditional approaches can be modularized. Typically, such an approach includes both a process and a language. The process takes as input requirements and produces a design model. The produced design model represents separate concerns and their relationships. The language provides constructs that can describe the elements to be represented in the design and the relationships that can exist between those elements. In particular, constructs are provided to support concern modularization and the specification of concern composition, with consideration for conflicts. Beyond that, the design of each individual modularized concern compares to standard software design.

Here, specific areas of excellence areas are:

- The aspect-oriented design process itself,

- The aspect-oriented design notations,

- Aspect-oriented design tool support,

- Adoption and integration of aspect-oriented design, and

- Assessment/evaluation of aspect-oriented design.

Aspect-oriented Programming (AOP)

AOP includes programming techniques and tools that support the modularization of concerns at the level of the source code. Just like any other programming language, an aspect-oriented language typically consists of two parts: a language specification and an implementation. Hence, there are two corresponding areas of concern: support for language developers and support for application developers.

Support for Application Developers

An aspect-oriented approach supports the implementation of concerns and how to compose those independently implemented concerns. While the specification of such a language is the primary manual for application developers, it provides obviously no guarantee that the application developer will produce high-quality aspect-oriented programs. Specific areas of excellence:

- The crucial concepts of aspect-oriented programming,

- Programming in aspect-oriented languages,

- Composing software components written in any language using aspect-oriented composition mechanisms, or

- Aspect-oriented programming environments.

Support for Language Developers

Excellence in constructing aspect-oriented languages includes the following areas:

- Constructing languages or dsls for specific domains and/or platforms, and

- Transferring implementation principles from other aspect-oriented execution environments, including:

  ◦ Interpreters,

  ◦ Compilers, and

  ◦ Virtual machines.

Formal Method Support for Aspect-orientation

Formal methods can be used both to define aspects semantically and to analyze and verify aspect-oriented systems. Aspect-oriented programming extends programming notations with aspect modules that isolate the declaration of when the aspect should be applied (join points) and what actions should be taken when it is reached (advice). Expertise in formal semantic definitions of aspect constructs is useful for language designers to provide a deep understanding of the differences among constructs. Aspects potentially can harm the reliability of a system to which they are woven, and could invalidate essential properties that already were true of the system without the aspect. It is also necessary to show that they actually do add intended crosscutting properties to the system.

Hence, numerous questions of correctness and verification are raised by aspect languages. Among the kinds of expertise are:

- Specially designed testing techniques to provide coverage for aspects,

- Program slicing and code analysis approaches to identify interactions among aspects and between aspects and underlying systems,

- Model checking techniques specialized for aspects, and

- Inductive techniques to verify aspect-oriented systems.

Each of the above approaches can be used to:

- Specify and analyze individual aspects relative to an existing system,

- Define conditions for composing multiple aspects correctly, and

- Detect and resolve potential interferences among aspects.

Although some approaches are already used in aspect languages, others are still subject of research and are not ready for routine industrial application. Nevertheless, awareness of these issues is essential for language designers, and for effective use of aspects, especially in safety-critical contexts.

Aspect-oriented Middleware

Middleware and AOSD strongly complement each other. In general, areas of excellence consist of:

- Support for the application developer, which includes:

  ○ The crucial concepts of aspect supporting middleware,

  ○ Aspect-oriented software development using a specific middleware, involving the aspect programming model, aspect deployment model, platform infrastructure, and services of the middleware, and

- Product family engineering (methods, architectures, techniques) in distributed and ambient computing, and

- Support for the middleware developer with respect to:

  ○ Host-infrastructure middleware,

  ○ Distribution middleware,

  ○ Common middleware services, and

  ○ Domain-specific middleware services.

Adoption

- IBM WebSphere Application Server (WAS) is a java application server that supports Java EE and Web Services. Websphere is distributed according to editions that support different features. Websphere uses AspectJ internally to isolate features of the different editions.

- JBoss Application Server (JBoss AS) is a free, open-source java application server that supports Java EE. The core of JBoss AS is integrated with the JBoss AOP aspect-oriented programming language. The application server uses JBoss AOP to deploy services such as security and transaction management.

- Oracle TopLink is a Java object-to-relational persistence framework that is integrated with the Spring Application Server. TopLink achieves high levels of persistence transparency using Spring AOP.

- SAP

- Sun Microsystems uses AspectJ to streamline mobile application development for the Java ME platform. Aspects are used to simplify the development of mobile applications for deployment to different operator decks and different mobile gaming community interfaces.

- Siemens Soarian is a health information management system that supports seamless access to patient medical records and the definition of workflows for health provider organizations. Soarian uses AspectJ to integrate crosscutting features such as tracing, auditing and performance monitoring in the context of an agile development process.

- Motorola wi4 is a cellular infrastructure system that provides support for the WiMAX wireless broadband standard. The wi4 control software is developed using an aspect-oriented extension to the UML 2.0 standard called WEAVR. WEAVR is used during the development for debugging and testing purposes.

- ASML is a provider of lithography systems for the semiconductor industry. ASML uses an aspect-oriented extension to C called Mirjam to modularize tracing and profiling concerns.

- Glassbox is a troubleshooting agent for Java applications that automatically diagnoses common problems. The Glassbox inspector monitors the activity of the Java virtual machine using AspectJ.

- .NET 3.5 supports Aspect Oriented concepts through the Unity container.

SOFTWARE DEVELOPMENT EFFORT ESTIMATION

In software development, effort estimation is the process of predicting the most realistic amount of effort (expressed in terms of person-hours or money) required to develop or maintain software based on incomplete, uncertain and noisy input. Effort estimates may be used as input to project plans, iteration plans, budgets, investment analyses, pricing processes and bidding rounds.

State-of-practice

Published surveys on estimation practice suggest that expert estimation is the dominant strategy when estimating software development effort. Typically, effort estimates are over-optimistic and there is a strong over-confidence in their accuracy. The mean effort overrun seems to be about 30% and not decreasing over time. However, the measurement of estimation error is problematic, The strong overconfidence in the accuracy of the effort estimates is illustrated by the finding that, on average, if a software professional is 90% confident or "almost sure" to include the actual effort in a minimum-maximum interval, the observed frequency of including the actual effort is only 60-70%.

Currently the term "effort estimate" is used to denote as different concepts such as most likely use of effort (modal value), the effort that corresponds to a probability of 50% of not exceeding (median), the planned effort, the budgeted effort or the effort used to propose a bid or price to the client. This is believed to be unfortunate, because communication problems may occur and because the concepts serve different goals.

Estimation Approaches

There are many ways of categorizing estimation approaches, The top level categories are the following:

- Expert estimation: The quantification step, i.e., the step where the estimate is produced based on judgmental processes.

- Formal estimation model: The quantification step is based on mechanical processes, e.g., the use of a formula derived from historical data.

- Combination-based estimation: The quantification step is based on a judgmental and mechanical combination of estimates from different sources.

Below are examples of estimation approaches within each category:

Estimation approach	Category	Examples of support of implementation of estimation approach
Analogy-based estimation	Formal estimation model	ANGEL, Weighted Micro Function Points
WBS-based (bottom up) estimation	Expert estimation	Project management software, company specific activity templates
Parametric models	Formal estimation model	COCOMO, SLIM, SEER-SEM, TruePlanning for Software
Size-based estimation models	Formal estimation model	Function Point Analysis, Use Case Analysis, Use Case Points, SSU (Software Size Unit), Story points-based estimation in Agile software development, Object Points
Group estimation	Expert estimation	Planning poker, Wideband delphi
Mechanical combination	Combination-based estimation	Average of an analogy-based and a Work breakdown structure-based effort estimate
Judgmental combination	Combination-based estimation	Expert judgment based on estimates from a parametric model and group estimation

Selection of Estimation Approaches

The evidence on differences in estimation accuracy of different estimation approaches and models suggest that there is no "best approach" and that the relative accuracy of one approach or model in comparison to another depends strongly on the context . This implies that different organizations benefit from different estimation approaches. Findings that may support the selection of estimation approach based on the expected accuracy of an approach include:

- Expert estimation is on average at least as accurate as model-based effort estimation. In particular, situations with unstable relationships and information of high importance not included in the model may suggest use of expert estimation. This assumes, of course, that experts with relevant experience are available.

- Formal estimation models not tailored to a particular organization's own context, may be very inaccurate. Use of own historical data is consequently crucial if one cannot be sure that the estimation model's core relationships (e.g., formula parameters) are based on similar project contexts.

- Formal estimation models may be particularly useful in situations where the model is tailored to the organization's context (either through use of own historical data or that the model is derived from similar projects and contexts), and it is likely that the experts' estimates will be subject to a strong degree of wishful thinking.

The most robust finding, in many forecasting domains, is that combination of estimates from independent sources, preferable applying different approaches, will on average improve the estimation accuracy. It is important to be aware of the limitations of each traditional approach to measuring software development productivity.

In addition, other factors such as ease of understanding and communicating the results of an approach, ease of use of an approach, and cost of introduction of an approach should be considered in a selection process.

Assessing the Accuracy of Estimates

The most common measure of the average estimation accuracy is the MMRE (Mean Magnitude of Relative Error), where the MRE of each estimate is defined as:

$$MRE = \frac{|\text{actual effort} - \text{estimated effort}|}{\text{actual effort}}$$

This measure has been criticized and there are several alternative measures, such as more symmetric measures, Weighted Mean of Quartiles of relative errors (WMQ) and Mean Variation from Estimate (MVFE).

MRE is not reliable if the individual items are skewed. PRED is preferred as a measure of estimation accuracy. PRED measures the percentage of predicted values that are within 25 percent of the actual value. A high estimation error cannot automatically be interpreted as an indicator of low estimation ability. Alternative, competing or complementing, reasons include low cost control of project, high complexity of development work, and more delivered functionality than originally estimated. A framework for improved use and interpretation of estimation error measurement is included in.

SOFTWARE DEVELOPMENTAL TOOLS

Tools used in the software development process can literally make or break a project. Once the target environment and programming language(s) is chosen, and the requirements and end goals are well-enough understood, the next task in starting the work of a software development project is to choose the tools that will be used throughout the process. It's important to be aware of the types of tools that are available for use, the benefits each can provide as well as the implications for using them.

Types of Software Development Tools

There are a variety of tools available to aid in the software development process. While this is by no means an exhaustive list of all the tools available in all environments, some of the most important categories of tools are:

Integrated Debugging Environment (IDE)

The IDE is where most developers spend the majority of their day working. It serves as a combination code editor and debugging interface. The IDE is also an integration point for many other types of tools.

Build Tools

Build tools include not just the compiler and link editor that translates the human-readable programming language statements into machine-executable instructions, but also the capabilities of managing dependencies.

Tools to Support Methodology

Some software development methodologies lend themselves to tools that make it easier to conform to the rules and guidelines imposed by the methodology. For example, tools exist that allow teams to organize use cases or user stories into time-bracketed sprints and track progress in addressing them over time.

Source Control

Managing access to the source code of the project is critical in the day-to-day work of any programming team. Concurrency must be managed so that one developer's changes don't overwrite other developers' work. Also, source control is extremely useful for creating branches/variations of the source, and merging changes between the branches. It also provides versioning and archive access to the source code as it changes over time.

Bug Trackers

Bug tracking is essential to ensuring that defects found during (and after) the development process are addressed and then re-tested. Bug trackers are often used as a primary interface with Quality Assurance.

Profilers

A variety of tools exist to report on the resource utilization of a program. Profilers can analyze memory usage, input/output, and processor usage in order to help developers detect and react to problems in the way their code is executing.

Automated Deployment/Continuous Integration Tools

Modern applications can be complex to deploy. Automating (or partially-automating) this function can reduce errors and save time. By employing a policy of continuous integration, problems in integrating the various components and features worked on by each developer can be spotted quickly and then addressed while it's still fresh in the developer's mind.

Testing Tools

Testing a software product is a key activity in assuring that it meets the requirements and is free of defects. Often it is desirable (or even policy) to create a test for every function in the program, and to run that test each time the function is modified to ensure that it produces the expected output and is free from any harmful side effects. In addition to this low-level "unit testing", testing of the program at the user interface level is necessary. Tools exist to assist in many different types of testing, and can often automate or partially-automate the task of performing each test.

Factors to Consider

There are several factors to consider when deciding which tools to utilize to aid in the development of a software project. Not all tools are necessarily appropriate for a given project, while others might be critical. Each team should consider a number of factors when deciding on the tools to use in the software development of each project.

Usefulness

The primary factor when deciding on whether to use a type of tool, and which implementation of that tool is the usefulness it will provide to the overall completion of the project.

Applicability to Environment

Not all tools apply to all environments. For example, a Windows desktop application will have no use for a web deployment tool.

Company Standards

In larger organizations, and often in smaller ones as well, use of certain tools will be mandated in order to achieve goals or to comply with established policy. Standardization of tools can help an organization move developers easily between projects as needed, and gives management an assurance that similar processes are followed among different project and project teams resulting in homogeneous product quality.

Prior Team Experience with Tool

To some degree, almost all software has a learning curve. The selection of specific tools can be influenced by the level of experience developers may already have with it. That specific experience can also be used as a resource in deciding whether a tool might be useful in the project or not, as developers usually form strong opinions on such matters and are usually not shy about expressing them.

Integration

How well a tool integrates into other tools can greatly impact the value it adds to the team and the project. Some Integration takes the form of "convenience" integration (i.e., the source control utility integrates with the IDE such that a developer automatically causes a file to be checked out once he begins editing it). Other deeper integration merges information and responds to events between tools to deliver high value to the team and to other groups within the organization. An example of this deeper integration is where source control integrates with bug tracking which in turn integrates with incident (or customer problem) tracking. A code change checked in to source control can signal the bug tracker that a fix is available for a reported bug; that bug may be associated with an incident report, which can then be updated with the status of the work that has been done that could (eventually) resolve that incident.

Overhead

All software has a learning curve, to one degree or another. Complex tools can also require time and effort to deploy with the team and integrate into existing development software. In addition to initial deployment and learning curve, many tools take some amount of time and effort to use. This overhead should be taken into account when evaluating the overall value of the tool.

References

- Molokken, K. Jorgensen, M. (2003). "A review of software surveys on software effort estimation". 2003 International Symposium on Empirical Software Engineering, 2003. ISESE 2003. Proceedings. pp. 223–230. doi:10.1109/ISESE.2003.1237981. ISBN 978-0-7695-2002-5

- Software-development, definition-16431: techopedia.com, Retrieved 15 July, 2019

- Shepperd, M. Kadoda, G. (2001). "Comparing software prediction techniques using simulation". IEEE Transactions on Software Engineering. 27 (11): 1014–1022. doi:10.1109/32.965341

- Software-development-process, careerfields, acqnote: acqnotes.com, Retrieved 08 May, 2019

- Bentley, Jon (1985). "Programming pearls". Communications of the ACM (fee required). 28 (9): 896–901. doi:10.1145/4284.315122. ISSN 0001-0782

- Software-requirement, software-engineering: ecomputernotes.com, Retrieved 11 April, 2019

Software Testing

The investigation which is conducted in order to provide stakeholders with information regarding the quality of the software product is known as software testing. Some of the methods of testing software are functional testing, non-functional testing and operational acceptance testing. The topics elaborated in this chapter will help in gaining a better perspective about these methods of software testing.

Software testing is defined as an activity to check whether the actual results match the expected results and to ensure that the software system is Defect free. It involves execution of a software component or system component to evaluate one or more properties of interest.

Software testing also helps to identify errors, gaps or missing requirements in contrary to the actual requirements. It can be either done manually or using automated tools. Some prefer saying Software testing as a White Box and Black Box Testing.

In simple terms, Software Testing means Verification of Application under Test (AUT).

Importance of Software Testing

Testing is important because software bugs could be expensive or even dangerous. Software bugs can potentially cause monetary and human loss, and history is full of such examples.

- In April 2015, Bloomberg terminal in London crashed due to software glitch affected more than 300,000 traders on financial markets. It forced the government to postpone a 3bn pound debt sale.

- Nissan cars have to recall over 1 million cars from the market due to software failure in the airbag sensory detectors. There have been reported two accidents due to this software failure.

- Starbucks was forced to close about 60 percent of stores in the U.S and Canada due to software failure in its POS system. At one point store served coffee for free as they unable to process the transaction.

- Some of the Amazon's third party retailers saw their product price is reduced to 1p due to a software glitch. They were left with heavy losses.

- Vulnerability in Window 10. This bug enables users to escape from security sandboxes through a flaw in the win32k system.

- In 2015 fighter plane F-35 fell victim to a software bug, making it unable to detect targets correctly.

- China Airlines Airbus A300 crashed due to a software bug on April 26, 1994, killing 264 innocent live

- In 1985, Canada's Therac-25 radiation therapy machine malfunctioned due to software bug and delivered lethal radiation doses to patients, leaving 3 people dead and critically injuring 3 others.

- In April of 1999, a software bug caused the failure of a $1.2 billion military satellite launch, the costliest accident in history.

- In May of 1996, a software bug caused the bank accounts of 823 customers of a major U.S. bank to be credited with 920 million US dollars.

Types of Software Testing

Typically Testing is classified into three categories.

- Functional Testing

- Non-Functional Testing or Performance Testing

- Maintenance (Regression and Maintenance).

Testing Category	Types of Testing
Functional Testing	<ul><li>Unit Testing</li><li>Integration Testing</li><li>Smoke</li><li>UAT(User Acceptance Testing)</li><li>Localization</li><li>Globalization</li><li>Interoperability</li><li>So on</li></ul>
Non-Functional Testing	<ul><li>Performance</li><li>Endurance</li><li>Load</li><li>Volume</li><li>Scalability</li><li>Usability</li><li>So on</li></ul>
Maintenance	<ul><li>Regression</li><li>Maintenance</li></ul>

FUNCTIONAL TESTING

Functional Testing is defined as a type of testing which verifies that each function of the software application operates in conformance with the requirement specification. This testing mainly involves black box testing and it is not concerned about the source code of the application.

Each and every functionality of the system is tested by providing appropriate input, verifying the output and comparing the actual results with the expected results.

This testing involves checking of User Interface, APIs, Database, security, client/ server applications and functionality of the Application under Test. The testing can be done either manually or using automation.

What do you Test in Functional Testing?

The prime objective of Functional testing is checking the functionalities of the software system. It mainly concentrates on:

- Mainline functions: Testing the main functions of an application.

- Basic Usability: It involves basic usability testing of the system. It checks whether a user can freely navigate through the screens without any difficulties.

- Accessibility: Checks the accessibility of the system for the user.

- Error Conditions: Usage of testing techniques to check for error conditions. It checks whether suitable error messages are displayed.

How to Perform Functional Testing: Complete Process

In order to functionally test an application, the following steps must be observed.

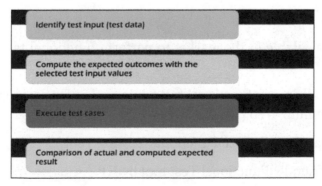

- Understand the Software Engineering Requirements.

- Identify test input (test data).

- Compute the expected outcomes with the selected test input values.

- Execute test cases.

- Comparison of actual and computed expected result.

Functional vs. Non-Functional Testing

Functional Testing	Non-Functional Testing
Functional testing is performed using the functional specification provided by the client and verifies the system against the functional requirements.	Non-Functional testing checks the Performance, reliability, scalability and other non-functional aspects of the software system.
Functional testing is executed first.	Non-functional testing should be performed after functional testing.
Manual Testing or automation tools can be used for functional testing.	Using tools will be effective for this testing.
Business requirements are the inputs to functional testing.	Performance parameters like speed, scalability are inputs to non-functional testing.
Functional testing describes what the product does.	Nonfunctional testing describes how good the product works.
Easy to do Manual Testing.	Tough to do Manual Testing.
Examples of Functional testing are: • Unit Testing • Smoke Testing • Sanity Testing • Integration Testing • White box testing • Black Box testing • User Acceptance testing • Regression Testing.	Examples of Non-functional testing are: • Performance Testing • Load Testing • Volume Testing • Stress Testing • Security Testing • Installation Testing • Penetration Testing • Compatibility Testing • Migration Testing.

Functional Testing Tools

There are several tools available in the market to perform functional testing. They are explained as follows:

- Ranorex Studio: all-in-one functional tests automation for desktop, web, and mobile apps with built-in Selenium Web Driver.

- Selenium: Popular Open Source Functional Testing Tool.

- QTP: Very user-friendly Functional Test tool by HP.

- JUnit: Used mainly for Java applications and this can be used in Unit and System Testing.

- soapUI: This is an open source functional testing tool, mainly used for Web service testing. It supports multiple protocols such as HTTP, SOAP, and JDBC.

- Watir: This is a functional testing tool for web applications. It supports tests executed at the web browser and uses a ruby scripting language.

NON FUNCTIONAL TESTING

Non-functional testing is defined as a type of Software testing to check non-functional aspects (performance, usability, reliability, etc) of a software application. It is designed to test the readiness of a system as per nonfunctional parameters which are never addressed by functional testing.

An excellent example of non-functional test would be to check how many people can simultaneously login into software. Non-functional testing is equally important as functional testing and affects client satisfaction.

Objectives of Non-functional Testing

- Non-functional testing should increase usability, efficiency, maintainability, and portability of the product.

- Helps to reduce production risk and cost associated with non-functional aspects of the product.

- Optimize the way product is installed, setup, executes, managed and monitored.

- Collect and produce measurements, and metrics for internal research and development.

- Improve and enhance knowledge of the product behavior and technologies in use.

Characteristics of Non-functional Testing

- Non-functional testing should be measurable, so there is no place for subjective characterization like good, better, best, etc.

- Exact numbers are unlikely to be known at the start of the requirement process.

- Important to prioritize the requirements.

- Ensure that quality attributes are identified correctly in Software Engineering.

Non-functional Testing Parameters

Non functional testing parameters.

1. Security: The parameter defines how a system is safeguarded against deliberate and sudden attacks from internal and external sources. This is tested via Security Testing.

2. Reliability: The extent to which any software system continuously performs the specified functions without failure. This is tested by Reliability Testing.

3. Survivability: The parameter checks that the software system continues to function and recovers itself in case of system failure. This is checked by Recovery Testing.

4. Availability: The parameter determines the degree to which user can depend on the system during its operation. This is checked by Stability Testing.

5. Usability: The ease with which the user can learn, operate, prepare inputs and outputs through interaction with a system. This is checked by Usability Testing.

6. Scalability: The term refers to the degree in which any software application can expand its processing capacity to meet an increase in demand. This is tested by Scalability Testing.

7. Interoperability: This non-functional parameter checks a software system interfaces with other software systems. This is checked by Interoperability Testing.

8. Efficiency: The extent to which any software system can handles capacity, quantity and response time.

9. Flexibility: The term refers to the ease with which the application can work in different hardware and software configurations. Like minimum RAM, CPU requirements.

10. Portability: The flexibility of software to transfer from its current hardware or software environment.

11. Reusability: It refers to a portion of the software system that can be converted for use in another application.

OPERATIONAL ACCEPTANCE TESTING

Operational Acceptance Testing (OAT) is a type of software testing that is performed to conduct operational pre-release of a software, system or application to check the quality of it. Operational Acceptance Testing is very usual software testing whose type is non-functional and it is mainly used in software development and software maintenance projects.

Operational Acceptance Testing mainly focuses on the operational readiness of the software and to become part of the production environment. Functional testing in operational acceptance testing is limited to the tests required to verify the non-functional aspects of the system.

Operational Acceptance Testing is also known as Operational Readiness Testing (ORT) or Operations Readiness and Assurance Testing (ORAT).

Objective of Operational Acceptance Testing

The objective of Operational Acceptance Testing is:

- To determine resiliency of the software.

- To determine recovering ability of the software.

- To determine integrity of the software.

- To determine software can be deployed on a network on ITIL standards.

- To determine supportability of the software.

Operational Acceptance Testing Steps

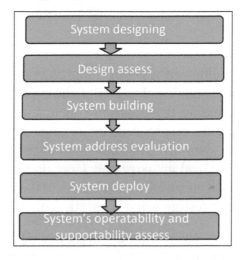

- System designing: First step is designing the system as per the user requirements. The system is designed in such a way that it fulfills the end user requirements.

- Design assess: After the designing of the system, its designing is analyzed. It is analyzed that whether the system is according to user requirements and whether it will operate the way it is designed.

- System building: After the design of system is prepared and analysis is done, system construction phase starts. It is the main phase of operational acceptance testing.

- System address evaluation: Once the system building is finished, after that system address is evaluated and it is checked whether is according to user requirement.

- System deploy: After building and address evaluation of software, it is established according to perform the specific task for the purpose of which it is constructed.

- System's operability and supportability assess: Now in the last phase the operability and supportability of the software system or application is tested. This leads to the end of whole procedure.

Types of Operational Acceptance Testing

- Load Testing

- Performance Testing

- Installation Testing

- Backup and Restore Testing
- Security Testing
- Recovery Testing.

Load Testing

Load testing is the process of putting demand on a system and measuring its response.

Software Load Testing

The term load testing is used in different ways in the professional software testing community. Load testing generally refers to the practice of modeling the expected usage of a software program by simulating multiple users accessing the program concurrently. As such, this testing is most relevant for multi-user systems; often one built using a client/server model, such as web servers. However, other types of software systems can also be load tested. For example, a word processor or graphics editor can be forced to read an extremely large document; or a financial package can be forced to generate a report based on several years' worth of data. The most accurate load testing simulates actual use, as opposed to testing using theoretical or analytical modeling.

Load testing lets you measure your website's quality of service (QOS) performance based on actual customer behavior. Nearly all the load testing tools and frame-works follow the classical load testing paradigm: when customers visit your web site, a script recorder records the communication and then creates related interaction scripts. A load generator tries to replay the recorded scripts, which could possibly be modified with different test parameters before replay. In the replay procedure, both the hardware and software statistics will be monitored and collected by the conductor, these statistics include the CPU, memory, disk IO of the physical servers and the response time, throughput of the system under test (SUT), etc. And at last, all these statistics will be analyzed and a load testing report will be generated.

Load and performance testing analyzes software intended for a multi-user audience by subjecting the software to different numbers of virtual and live users while monitoring performance measurements under these different loads. Load and performance testing is usually conducted in a test environment identical to the production environment before the software system is permitted to go live.

As an example, a web site with shopping cart capability is required to support 100 concurrent users broken out into following activities:

- 25 virtual users (VUsers) log in, browse through items and then log off.
- 25 VUsers log in, add items to their shopping cart, check out and then log off.
- 25 VUsers log in, return items previously purchased and then log off.
- 25 VUsers just log in without any subsequent activity.

A test analyst can use various load testing tools to create these VUsers and their activities. Once the test has started and reached a steady state, the application is being tested at the 100 VUser load as described above. The application's performance can then be monitored and captured.

The specifics of a load test plan or script will generally vary across organizations. For example, in the bulleted list above, the first item could represent 25 VUsers browsing unique items, random items, or a selected set of items depending upon the test plan or script developed. However, all load test plans attempt to simulate system performance across a range of anticipated peak workflows and volumes. The criteria for passing or failing a load test (pass/fail criteria) are generally different across organizations as well. There are no standards specifying acceptable load testing performance metrics.

A common misconception is that load testing software provides record and playback capabilities like regression testing tools. Load testing tools analyze the entire OSI protocol stack whereas most regression testing tools focus on GUI performance. For example, a regression testing tool will record and playback a mouse click on a button on a web browser, but a load testing tool will send out hypertext the web browser sends after the user clicks the button. In a multiple-user environment, load testing tools can send out hypertext for multiple users with each user having a unique login ID, password, etc.

The popular load testing tools available also provide insight into the causes for slow performance. There are numerous possible causes for slow system performance, including, but not limited to, the following:

- Application server(s) or software.

- Database server(s).

- Network – latency, congestion, etc.

- Client-side processing.

- Load balancing between multiple servers.

Load testing is especially important if the application, system or service will be subject to a service level agreement or SLA.

Load testing is performed to determine a system's behavior under both normal and anticipated peak load conditions. It helps to identify the maximum operating capacity of an application as well as any bottlenecks and determine which element is causing degradation. When the load placed on the system is raised beyond normal usage patterns to test the system's response at unusually high or peak loads, it is known as stress testing. The load is usually so great that error conditions are the expected result, but there is no clear boundary when an activity ceases to be a load test and becomes a stress test.

The term "load testing" is often used synonymously with concurrency testing, software performance testing, reliability testing, and volume testing for specific scenarios. All of these are types of non-functional testing that are not part of functionality testing used to validate suitability for use of any given software.

User Experience under Load Test

In the example above, while the device under test (DUT) is under production load - 100 VUsers, run the target application. The performance of the target application here would be the user experience under load. It describes how fast or slow the DUT responds, and how satisfied or how the user actually perceives performance.

Browser-level vs. Protocol-level Users

Historically, all load testing was performed with automated API tests that simulated traffic through concurrent interactions at the protocol layer (often called protocol level users or PLUs). With the advance of containers and cloud infrastructure, the option is now present to test with real browsers (often called browser level users or BLUs). Each approach has its merits for different types of applications, but generally browser-level users will be more akin to the real traffic that a website will experience and provide a more realistic load profile and response time measurement. BLUs are certainly a more expensive way of running tests and cannot work with all types of applications, specifically those that are not accessible through a web browser like a desktop client or API-based application.

Physical Load Testing

Many types of machinery, engines, structures, and motors are load tested. The load may be at a designated safe working load (SWL), full load, or at an aggravated level of load. The governing contract, technical specification or test method contains the details of conducting the test. The purpose of a mechanical load test is to verify that all the component parts of a structure including materials, base-fixings are fit for task and loading it is designed for.

Several types of load testing are employed:

- Static testing is when a designated constant load is applied for a specified time.

- Dynamic testing is when a variable or moving load is applied.

- Cyclical testing consists of repeated loading and unloading for specified cycles, durations and conditions.

The Supply of Machinery (Safety) Regulation 1992 UK state that load testing is undertaken before the equipment is put into service for the first time. Performance testing applies a safe working load (SWL), or other specified load, for a designated time in a governing test method, specification, or contract. Under the Lifting Operations and Lifting Equipment Regulations 1998 UK load testing after the initial test is required if a major component is replaced, if the item is moved from one location to another or as dictated by the competent person.

Software Performance Testing

Performance Testing is defined as a type of software testing to ensure software applications will perform well under their expected workload.

Features and Functionality supported by a software system is not the only concern. A software application's performance like its response time, reliability, resource usage and scalability do matter. The goal of Performance Testing is not to find bugs but to eliminate performance bottlenecks.

The focus of Performance Testing is checking a software program's:

- Speed - Determines whether the application responds quickly.

- Scalability - Determines maximum user load the software application can handle.

- Stability - Determines if the application is stable under varying loads.

Performance Testing is popularly called "Perf Testing" and is a subset of performance engineering.

Need of Performance Testing

Performance Testing is done to provide stakeholders with information about their application regarding speed, stability, and scalability. More importantly, Performance Testing uncovers what needs to be improved before the product goes to market. Without Performance Testing, software is likely to suffer from issues such as: running slow while several users use it simultaneously, inconsistencies across different operating systems and poor usability.

Performance testing will determine whether their software meets speed, scalability and stability requirements under expected workloads. Applications sent to market with poor performance metrics due to nonexistent or poor performance testing are likely to gain a bad reputation and fail to meet expected sales goals.

Also, mission-critical applications like space launch programs or life-saving medical equipment should be performance tested to ensure that they run for a long period without deviations.

According to Dunn & Bradstreet, 59% of Fortune 500 companies experience an estimated 1.6 hours of downtime every week. Considering the average Fortune 500 company with a minimum of 10,000 employees is paying $56 per hour, the labor part of downtime costs for such an organization would be $896,000 weekly, translating into more than $46 million per year.

Only a 5-minute downtime of Google.com (19-Aug-13) is estimated to cost the search giant as much as $545,000. It's estimated that companies lost sales worth $1100 per second due to a recent Amazon Web Service Outage. Hence, performance testing is important.

Types of Performance Testing

- Load testing - Checks the application's ability to perform under anticipated user loads. The objective is to identify performance bottlenecks before the software application goes live.

- Stress testing -Involves testing an application under extreme workloads to see how it handles high traffic or data processing. The objective is to identify the breaking point of an application.

- Endurance testing - Is done to make sure the software can handle the expected load over a long period of time.

- Spike testing - Tests the software's reaction to sudden large spikes in the load generated by users.

- Volume testing - Under Volume Testing large no. of. Data is populated in a database and the overall software system's behavior is monitored. The objective is to check software application's performance under varying database volumes.

- Scalability testing - The objective of scalability testing is to determine the software application's effectiveness in "scaling up" to support an increase in user load. It helps plan capacity addition to your software system.

Common Performance Problems

Most performance problems revolve around speed, response time, load time and poor scalability. Speed is often one of the most important attributes of an application. A slow running application will lose potential users. Performance testing is done to make sure an app runs fast enough to keep a user's attention and interest. Take a look at the following list of common performance problems and notice how speed is a common factor in many of them:

- Long Load time - Load time is normally the initial time it takes an application to start. This should generally be kept to a minimum. While some applications are impossible to make load in under a minute, Load time should be kept under a few seconds if possible.

- Poor response time - Response time is the time it takes from when a user inputs data into the application until the application outputs a response to that input. Generally, this should be very quick. Again if a user has to wait too long, they lose interest.

- Poor scalability - A software product suffers from poor scalability when it cannot handle the expected number of users or when it does not accommodate a wide enough range of users. Load Testing should be done to be certain the application can handle the anticipated number of users.

- Bottlenecking - Bottlenecks are obstructions in a system which degrade overall system performance. Bottlenecking is when either coding errors or hardware issues cause a decrease of throughput under certain loads. Bottlenecking is often caused by one faulty section of code. The key to fixing a bottlenecking issue is to find the section of code that is causing the slowdown and try to fix it there. Bottlenecking is generally fixed by either fixing poor running processes or adding additional Hardware. Some common performance bottlenecks are:

  - CPU utilization

  - Memory utilization

  - Network utilization

  - Operating System limitations

  - Disk usage.

Performance Testing Process

The methodology adopted for performance testing can vary widely but the objective for performance tests remain the same. It can help demonstrate that your software system meets certain pre-defined performance criteria. Or it can help compare the performance of two software systems. It can also help identify parts of your software system which degrade its performance.

Below is a generic process on how to perform performance testing:

1. Identify your testing environment - Know your physical test environment, production environment and what testing tools are available. Understand details of the hardware, software and network configurations used during testing before you begin the testing process. It will help testers create more efficient tests. It will also help identify possible challenges that testers may encounter during the performance testing procedures.

2. Identify the performance acceptance criteria - This includes goals and constraints for throughput, response times and resource allocation. It is also necessary to identify project success criteria outside of these goals and constraints. Testers should be empowered to set performance criteria and goals because often the project specifications will not include a wide enough variety of performance benchmarks. Sometimes there may be none at all. When possible finding a similar application to compare to is a good way to set performance goals.

3. Plan & design performance tests - Determine how usage is likely to vary amongst end users and identify key scenarios to test for all possible use cases. It is necessary to simulate a variety of end users, plan performance test data and outline what metrics will be gathered.

4. Configuring the test environment - Prepare the testing environment before execution. Also, arrange tools and other resources.

5. Implement test design - Create the performance tests according to your test design.

6. Run the tests - Execute and monitor the tests.

7. Analyze, tune and retest - Consolidate, analyze and share test results. Then fine tune and test again to see if there is an improvement or decrease in performance. Since improvements generally grow smaller with each retest, stop when bottlenecking is caused by the CPU. Then you may have the consider option of increasing CPU power.

Performance Testing Metrics: Parameters Monitored

The basic parameters monitored during performance testing include:

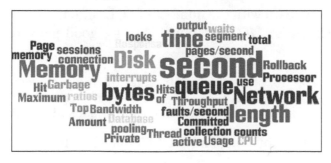

- Processor Usage - An amount of time processor spends executing non-idle threads.

- Memory use - Amount of physical memory available to processes on a computer.

- Disk time - Amount of time disk is busy executing a read or write request.

- Bandwidth - Shows the bits per second used by a network interface.

- Private bytes - Number of bytes a process has allocated that can't be shared amongst other processes. These are used to measure memory leaks and usage.

- Committed memory - Amount of virtual memory used.

- Memory pages/second - Number of pages written to or read from the disk in order to resolve hard page faults. Hard page faults are when code not from the current working set is called up from elsewhere and retrieved from a disk.

- Page faults/second - The overall rate in which fault pages are processed by the processor. This again occurs when a process requires code from outside its working set.

- CPU interrupts per second - Is the avg. number of hardware interrupts a processor is receiving and processing each second.

- Disk queue length - Is the avg. no. of read and write requests queued for the selected disk during a sample interval.

- Network output queue length - Length of the output packet queue in packets. Anything more than two means a delay and bottlenecking needs to be stopped.

- Network bytes total per second - Rate which bytes are sent and received on the interface including framing characters.

- Response time - Time from when a user enters a request until the first character of the response is received.

- Throughput - Rate a computer or network receives requests per second.

- Amount of connection pooling - The number of user requests that are met by pooled connections. The more requests met by connections in the pool, the better the performance will be.

- Maximum active sessions - The maximum number of sessions that can be active at once.

- Hit ratios - This has to do with the number of SQL statements that are handled by cached data instead of expensive I/O operations. This is a good place to start for solving bottlenecking issues.

- Hits per second - The no. of hits on a web server during each second of a load test.

- Rollback segment - The amount of data that can rollback at any point in time.

- Database locks - Locking of tables and databases needs to be monitored and carefully tuned.

- Top waits - Are monitored to determine what wait times can be cut down when dealing with the how fast data is retrieved from memory.

- Thread counts - An applications health can be measured by the no. of threads that are running and currently active.

- Garbage collection - It has to do with returning unused memory back to the system. Garbage collection needs to be monitored for efficiency.

Example Performance Test Cases

- Verify response time is not more than 4 secs when 1000 users access the website simultaneously.

- Verify response time of the Application Under Load is within an acceptable range when the network connectivity is slow.

- Check the maximum number of users that the application can handle before it crashes.

- Check database execution time when 500 records are read/written simultaneously.

- Check CPU and memory usage of the application and the database server under peak load conditions.

- Verify response time of the application under low, normal, moderate and heavy load conditions.

During the actual performance test execution, vague terms like acceptable range, heavy load, etc. are replaced by concrete numbers. Performance engineers set these numbers as per business requirements, and the technical landscape of the application.

Performance Test Tools

There are a wide variety of performance testing tools available in the market. The tool you choose for testing will depend on many factors such as types of the protocol supported, license cost, hardware requirements, platform support etc. Below is a list of popularly used testing tools:

- LoadNinja – is revolutionizing the way we load test. This cloud-based load testing tool empowers teams to record & instantly playback comprehensive load tests, without complex dynamic correlation & run these load tests in real browsers at scale. Teams are able to increase test coverage. & cut load testing time by over 60%.

- NeoLoad - is the performance testing platform designed for DevOps that seamlessly integrates into your existing Continuous Delivery pipeline. With NeoLoad, teams test 10x faster than with traditional tools to meet the new level of requirements across the full Agile software development lifecycle - from component to full system-wide load tests.

- HP LoadRunner - is the most popular performance testing tools on the market today. This tool is capable of simulating hundreds of thousands of users, putting applications under real-life loads to determine their behavior under expected loads. Loadrunner features a virtual user generator which simulates the actions of live human users.

- Jmeter - one of the leading tools used for load testing of web and application servers.

Installation Testing

Installation testing is to check that software application is successfully installed & it is working as expected after installation. This is testing phase prior to end users will firstly interact with the actual application. Installation testing is also called as "Implementation Testing". This is most important as well as most interesting step in the Software testing life cycle.

Few points need to check in the prior to Installation testing:

- Verify the pre-requisites needed to software install the application if any.

- Installation should be run at default location & it should present to user with default location with user can able to change the default location.

- Verify that user should able to install software from different location like over network, online installation, installation from CD etc.

- Verify software installation without giving the administrative privileges.

- Verify to check working of Installer.exe is executing smoothly on clean state.

- Verify to check is the Installer.exe is calculating the disk space needed to successfully install the application prior to install the application.

- Verify the software installation on multiple platforms, before doing this need to confirm the supported list of platforms.

- Verify that successful "Silent installation". In the Silent installation messages in the process of installation are not displayed on UI, all messages are added in log files and based on messages occurred is used as input in the installation process.

- Verify if the Interactive installation, GUI screen presented to user & user needs to provide input parameters in installation. This is majorly used in product installation.

- Verify that after successful installation of software is it working as per mention in specification document & meet user needs.

- Upon un-installation of software application check for the all previously installed files and registry entries are removed or not.

- Verify that is user able to uninstall or repair the software application.

Customer will happy on successful installation of software, Definitely yes. But you think of other way round if it fails to install. Upon failure of installation our software will not work but it might be possible that the data present on customers machine may affect badly. As a result, it makes bad impression on customer. This is due to the incomplete installer testing.

What all things you Need to make Good Impression on Customer?

The installation testing of software should be done on different platforms with manual or automated method. But to complete this time is the major concern. It is time consuming task & to execute a single test case on multiple platform might requires lots of time. And there are multiple test cases to execute.

Before starting the software installation test figure out on how many configurations installer needs to be supported. Make it one Hard Disk Drive (HDD) formatted. Install a new operating system on it. Add all pre-requisites required prior to install the software application. So it is ready to first install test on your newly prepared configuration. Wait, before going further make an image of your base HDD, so we will called as base image & it will be use for testing onward.

You can create a backup of base configuration (you can use Norton Ghost to make this copy, it's easy & fast). The copy of this base configuration will be used in each time of testing, it will save time a lot. Let's take a simple e.g. if 1 hour is required to make formatting of system & to make it new configuration. But by creating the image of base configuration will take hardly 10mins, here you are saving approximately 50 mins on each restoration of systemJ, so you can test it over multiple platforms with various scenarios in time. Make sure that the un-installation scenario also needs to be executed on different platform combination.

Installation Testing tips with Some broad Test Cases

1. Install full version of application: In case if you upgrading the application or previously installed a basic version now installing the full version on same path then system should allow you to install full version application without any error. Before installing newer version it should display a message on GUI saying old version is detected & do you want to continue.

2. Automate testing efforts: The flow chart below is useful to create the automated scripts, using this flow chart you can easily make out the automated script for installation testing.

3. After executing every test case use of disk image (created above) to be installing on dedicated machine which will save time.

4. Required disk space check in installation: This is most critical scenario in the installation testing. In the installation process check for "Is installer checking for minimum required disk space check prior to installation?" If for installing a software application the installer required space of 4MB then in the initial steps installer need to check whether the selected destination location have free space of 4MB at least to complete the installation. Also verify that the after successful installation, 4MB space is utilized by the installed system & if the more space is utilized then error should trigger.

The Disk space checking is done using automated and manual testing method. You can verify calculated disk space by installer is correct or not by using manually or automated tools.

5. On different file system format the disk space may vary like on NTFS, FAT32, and FAT16 etc. so this case should be grouped in multi-platform test cases.

6. Use of distributed testing environment: To executing test cases effectively you can use of distributed testing environment, which will save your cost & time. Using such master & slave model will help to execute different installation test cases on different platform simultaneously. Using distributed environment master model simultaneously trigger to salves for different platform & consolidated execution result collected at center location in Master model.

7. Automate the check of files installed after installation: You can use of automated script to check the all required file are got installed successfully. So you can use this script for checking completeness of installed application.

In manual methods you can check free disk space available on drive before installation and disk space reported by installer script to check whether installer is calculating and reporting disk space accurately.

8. Confirm for registry changes after installation: You have to check for registry changes after the installation of software. This is to check whether expected changes are reflected in registry files. In the market many registry checking software's are available for free.

9. Negative testing in installation testing: Intensely try to break the installation process to check the behavior of application under such condition. Such negative test cases should be executed on every step in Installation testing. The most important check is to confirm that state of system should change to original state.

Make it dedicated system for installation of software will help to save time & get testing complete in faster. Also check system behavior installation in low disk space conditions.

10. Uninstallation testing: You should also check for un-install testing to check whether the user is able to uninstall the application without any error & removing the all folders & files relate to installation. Also need confirm that not impacting the other working features in the system which was previously working fine.

Recovery Testing

Recovery testing is basically done in order to check how fast and better the application can recover against any type of crash or hardware failure etc. Type or extent of recovery is specified in the requirement specifications. It is basically testing how well a system recovers from crashes, hardware failures, or other catastrophic problems. Recovery testing is an effective way to check the recovery rate of an application when it has suffered a huge blow of hardware failure or crash. It is a way of manually stimulating the failure of the software to test the possibility and the rate of its recovery.

Recovery Testing in Software

There is an array of software testing to ensure its efficiency. One of these testing techniques is non-functional testing. A non-functional testing is a term used for the part of the software that is not connected to a specific user action or function such as security. This is further sub-divided into many testing methods among which is Recovery testing.

Recovery testing can be performed in a number of ways. Some practical examples of stimulating software failure to test its recovery ability are:

- While a system is receiving some data from a network for processing, you can stimulate software failure by unplugging the system. After some minutes, you can plug the system again and test the ability of the software to continue receiving the data after the brief interruption.

- When a browser is working on some sessions, you can restart the system to stimulate software failure. After restarting the system, check the browser whether it can automatically recover the opened sessions.

- If you are downloading music to your mobile device by using your data, move to a place where there is no network. The downloading will be interrupted. Move back to where there is network and see how it goes. If the downloading continues from where it stops, the system has a good recovery rate.

These are typical example of what recovery testing is and the recovery rate is determined by some factors such as:

- The volume of the tested application.

- The amount of the restart points.

- The skills of the recovery testers.

- The type of tools available to promote the recovery.

Recovery Process Cycle

The recovery process is expected to have five different steps:

- Normal operation

- Disaster occurrence

- Disruption of operation

- Clearing disaster through the recovery process

- Pulling together all the processes and information necessary to restore the software to normal.

A good software system is expected to seamlessly shift from one stage to the other without hitches to ensure that it has an acceptable recovery.

Instructions

Some precautionary measures should be taken before carrying out recovery testing on a software program. A couple of what should be considered are:

- A condition that is nearly identical to the real life situation should be created. Caution should be taken to ensure that the hardware, protocol, software, and firmware should be very close to the condition that is imitated.

- The complete checking of the system should be carried out as well as ensure that there is an identical configuration despite how expensive the process will be.

- The size of the backup is expected to be the same as the size of the original source of the information in some backup systems.

- An online backup may be a good backup idea to prevent total loss of information during recovery testing. However, it is important that you test the system's restore ability before carrying out the recovery testing on a particular software program.

Advantages of Recovery Testing

1. It eliminates risks: Recovery testing exposes potential flaws that can lead to the failure of the product when used by the end users.

2. It improves the quality of the system: After detecting a flaw, it will be corrected to ensure the system is working as expected. This leads to improved system quality.

This is a necessity for the efficiency of a software program.

Security Testing

Security Testing is defined as a type of Software Testing that ensures software systems and applications are free from any vulnerabilities, threats, risks that may cause a big loss. Security testing of any system is about finding all possible loopholes and weaknesses of the system which might result into a loss of information, revenue, repute at the hands of the employees or outsiders of the Organization.

The goal of security testing is to identify the threats in the system and measure its potential vulnerabilities, so the system does not stop functioning or is exploited. It also helps in detecting all possible security risks in the system and help developers in fixing these problems through coding.

Types of Security Testing

There are seven main types of security testing as per Open Source Security Testing methodology manual. They are explained as follows:

- Vulnerability Scanning: This is done through automated software to scan a system against known vulnerability signatures.

- Security Scanning: It involves identifying network and system weaknesses, and later provides solutions for reducing these risks. This scanning can be performed for both Manual and Automated scanning.

- Penetration Testing: This kind of testing simulates an attack from a malicious hacker. This testing involves analysis of a particular system to check for potential vulnerabilities to an external hacking attempt.

- Risk Assessment: This testing involves analysis of security risks observed in the organization. Risks are classified as Low, Medium and High. This testing recommends controls and measures to reduce the risk.

- Security Auditing: This is an internal inspection of Applications and Operating systems for security flaws. An audit can also be done via line by line inspection of code.

- Ethical Hacking: It's hacking an Organization Software systems. Unlike malicious hackers, who steal for their own gains, the intent is to expose security flaws in the system.

- Posture Assessment: This combines Security scanning, Ethical Hacking and Risk Assessments to show an overall security posture of an organization.

Process of Security Testing

It is always agreed, that cost will be more if we postpone security testing after software implementation phase or after deployment. So, it is necessary to involve security testing in the SDLC life cycle in the earlier phases.

Let's look into the corresponding Security processes to be adopted for every phase in SDLC.

SDLC Phases	Security Processes
Requirements	Security analysis for requirements and check abuse/misuse cases
Design	Security risks analysis for designing. Development of Test Plan including security tests
Coding and Unit Testing	Static and Dynamic Testing and Security White Box Testing
Integration Testing	Black Box Testing
System Testing	Black Box Testing and Vulnerability scanning
Implementation	Penetration Testing, Vulnerability Scanning
Support	Impact analysis of Patches

The test plan should include:

- Security-related test cases or scenarios
- Test Data related to security testing
- Test Tools required for security testing
- Analysis of various tests outputs from different security tools.

Example Test Scenarios for Security Testing

Sample Test scenarios to give you a glimpse of security test cases:

- A password should be in encrypted format
- Application or System should not allow invalid users
- Check cookies and session time for application
- For financial sites, the Browser back button should not work.

Methodologies/Approach/Techniques for Security Testing

In security testing, different methodologies are followed, and they are as follows:

- Tiger Box: This hacking is usually done on a laptop which has a collection of OSs and hacking tools. This testing helps penetration testers and security testers to conduct vulnerabilities assessment and attacks.

- Black Box: Tester is authorized to do testing on everything about the network topology and the technology.

- Grey Box: Partial information is given to the tester about the system, and it is a hybrid of white and black box models.

Security Testing Roles

- Hackers - Access computer system or network without authorization.

- Crackers - Break into the systems to steal or destroy data.

- Ethical Hacker - Performs most of the breaking activities but with permission from the owner.

- Script Kiddies or packet monkeys - Inexperienced Hackers with programming language skill.

Security Testing Tool

Owasp

The Open Web Application Security Project (OWASP) is a worldwide non-profit organization focused on improving the security of software. The project has multiple tools to pen test various software environments and protocols. Flagship tools of the project include:

1. Zed Attack Proxy (ZAP – an integrated penetration testing tool).

2. OWASP Dependency Check (it scans for project dependencies and checks against know vulnerabilities).

3. OWASP Web Testing Environment Project (collection of security tools and documentation).

WireShark

Wireshark is a network analysis tool previously known as Ethereal. It captures packet in real time and display them in human readable format. Basically, it is a network packet analyzer- which provides the minute details about your network protocols, decryption, packet information, etc. It is an open source and can be used on Linux, Windows, OS X, Solaris, NetBSD, FreeBSD and many other systems. The information that is retrieved via this tool can be viewed through a GUI or the TTY mode TShark Utility.

W3af

w3af is a web application attack and audit framework. It has three types of plugins; discovery, audit and attack that communicate with each other for any vulnerabilities in site, for example a discovery plugin in w3af looks for different url's to test for vulnerabilities and forward it to the audit plugin which then uses these URL's to search for vulnerabilities.

Recovery Testing

Recovery Testing is defined as a software testing type, that is performed to determine whether operations can be continued after a disaster or after the integrity of the system has been lost. It involves reverting to a point where the integrity of the system was known and then reprocessing transactions up to the point of failure. The purpose of recovery testing is to verify the system's ability to recover from varying points of failure.

Recovery Testing Example

When an application is receiving data from the network, unplug the connecting cable.

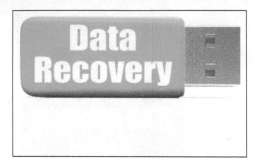

- After some time, plug the cable back in and analyze the application's ability to continue receiving data from the point at which the network connection was broken.

- Restart the system while a browser has a definite number of sessions open and check whether the browser is able to recover all of them or not.

In Software Engineering, Recoverability Testing is a type of Non- Functional Testing. (Non- functional testing refers to aspects of the software that may not be related to a specific function or user action such as scalability or security.)

The time taken to recover depends upon:

- The number of restart points

- A volume of the applications

- Training and skills of people conducting recovery activities and tools available for recovery.

When there are a number of failures then instead of taking care of all failures, the recovery testing should be done in a structured fashion which means recovery testing should be carried out for one segment and then another.

It is done by professional testers. Before recovery testing, adequate backup data is kept in secure locations. This is done to ensure that the operation can be continued even after a disaster.

Life Cycle of Recovery Process

The life cycle of the recovery process can be classified into the following five steps:

1. Normal operation: A system consisting of hardware, software, and firmware integrated to achieve a common goal is made operational for carrying out a well-defined and stated goal. The system is called to perform the normal operation to carry out the designed job without any disruption within a stipulated period of time.

2. Disaster occurrence: A disruption may occur due to malfunction of the software, due to various reasons like input initiated malfunction, software crashing due to hardware failure, damaged due to fire, theft, and strike.

3. Disruption and failure of the operation: Disruption phase is a most painful phase which leads to business losses, relation break, opportunity losses, man-hour losses and invariably financial and goodwill losses. Every sensible agency should have a plan for disaster recovery to enable the disruption phase to be minimal.

4. Disaster clearance through the recovery process: If a backup plan and risk mitigation processes are at the right place before encountering disaster and disruption, then recovery can be done without much loss of time, effort and energy. A designated individual, along with his team with the assigned role of each of these persons should be defined to fix the responsibility and help the organization to save from long disruption period.

5. Reconstruction of all processes and information to bring the whole system to move to normal operation: Reconstruction may involve multiple sessions of operation to rebuild all folders along with configuration files. There should be proper documentation and process of reconstruction for correct recovery.

Restoration Strategy

The recovery team should have their unique strategy for retrieving the important code and data to bring the operation of the agency back to normalcy.

The strategy can be unique to each organization based on the criticality of the systems they are handling. The possible strategy for critical systems can be visualized as follows:

1. To have a single backup or more than one.

2. To have multiple back-ups at one place or different places.

3. To have an online backup or offline backup.

4. Can the backup is done automatically based on a policy or to have it manually?

5. To have an independent restoration team or development team itself can be utilized for the work.

Each of these strategies has cost factor associated with it and multiple resources required for multiple back-ups may consume more physical resources or may need an independent team.

Many companies may be affected due to their data and code dependency on the concerned developer agency. For instance, if Amazon AWS goes down its shuts 25 of the internet. Independent Restoration is crucial in such cases.

How to do Recovery Testing

While performing recovery testing following things should be considered:

- We must create a test bed as close to actual conditions of deployment as possible. Changes in interfacing, protocol, firmware, hardware, and software should be as close to the actual condition as possible if not the same condition.

- Through exhaustive testing may be time-consuming and a costly affair, identical configuration, and complete check should be performed.

- If possible, testing should be performed on the hardware we are finally going to restore. This is especially true if we are restoring to a different machine than the one that created the backup.

- Some backup systems expect the hard drive to be exactly the same size as the one the backup was taken from.

- Obsolescence should be managed as drive technology is advancing at a fast pace, and old drive may not be compatible with the new one. One way to handle the problem is to restore to a virtual machine. Virtualization software vendors like VMware Inc. can configure virtual machines to mimic existing hardware, including disk sizes and other configurations.

- Online backup systems are not an exception for testing. Most online backup service providers protect us from being directly exposed to media problems by the way they use fault-tolerant storage systems.

- While online backup systems are extremely reliable, we must test the restore side of the system to make sure there are no problems with the retrieval functionality, security or encryption.

Testing Procedure after Restoration

Most large corporations have independent auditors to perform recovery test exercises periodically. The expense of maintaining and testing a comprehensive disaster recovery plan can be substantial, and it may be prohibitive for smaller businesses.

Smaller risks may rely on their data backups and off-site storage plans to save them in the case of a catastrophe. After folders and files are restored, following checks can be done to assure that files are recovered properly:

- Rename the corrupted document folder.

- Count the files in the restored folders and match with it with an existing folder.

- Open a few of the files and make sure they are accessible. Be sure to open them with the application that normally uses them. And make sure you can browse the data, update the data or whatever you normally do.

- It is best to open several files of different types, pictures, mp3s, documents and some large and some small.

- Most operating systems have utilities that you can use to compare files and directories.

SMOKE TESTING

Smoke testing is defined as a type of software testing that determines whether the deployed build is stable or not. This serves as confirmation whether the QA team can proceed with further testing. Smoke tests are a minimal set of tests run on each build. Here is the cycle where smoke testing is involved. Smoke testing is a process where the software build is deployed to QA environment and is verified to ensure the stability of the application. It is also called as "Build verification Testing" or "Confidence Testing."

In simple terms, we are verifying whether the important features are working and there are no showstoppers in the build that is under testing.

It is a mini and rapid regression test of major functionality. It is a simple test that shows the product is ready for testing. This helps determine if the build is flawed as to make any further testing a waste of time and resources.

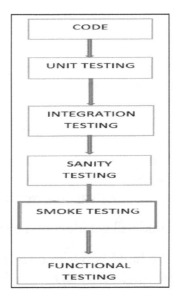

The smoke tests qualify the build for further formal testing. The main aim of smoke testing is to detect early major issues. Smoke tests are designed to demonstrate system stability and conformance to requirements.

A build includes all data files, libraries, reusable modules, engineered components that are required to implement one or more product functions.

When do we do Smoke Testing

Smoke Testing is done whenever the new functionalities of software are developed and integrated with existing build that is deployed in QA/staging environment. It ensures that all critical functionalities are working correctly or not.

In this testing method, the development team deploys the build in QA. The subsets of test cases are taken, and then testers run test cases on the build. The QA team test the application against the critical functionalities. These series of test cases are designed to expose errors that are in build. If these tests are passed, QA team continues with Functional Testing. Any failure indicates a need to handle the system back to the development team. Whenever there is a change in the build, we perform Smoke Testing to ensure the stability.

Example: New registration button is added in the login window and build is deployed with the new code. We perform smoke testing on a new build.

Who Performs Smoke Testing

After releasing the build to QA environment, Smoke Testing is performed by QA engineers/QA lead. Whenever there is a new build, QA team determines the major functionality in the application to perform smoke testing. QA team checks for showstoppers in the application that is under testing.

Testing done in a development environment on the code to ensure the correctness of the application before releasing build to QA, this is known as Sanity testing. It is usually narrow and deep testing. It is a process which verifies that the application under development meets its basic functional requirements.

Sanity testing determines the completion of the development phase and makes a decision whether to pass or not to pass software product for further testing phase.

Need of Smoke Testing

Smoke testing plays an important role in software development as it ensures the correctness of the system in initial stages. By this, we can save test effort. As a result, smoke tests bring the system to a good state. Once we complete smoke testing then only we start functional testing:

- All the show stoppers in the build will get identified by performing smoke testing.

- Smoke testing is done after the build is released to QA. With the help of smoke testing, most of the defects are identified at initial stages of software development.

- With smoke testing, we simplify the detection and correction of major defects.

- By smoke testing, QA team can find defects to the application functionality that may have surfaced by the new code.

- Smoke testing finds the major severity defects.

Examples:

- Logging window: Able to move to next window with valid username and password on clicking submit button.

- User unable to sign out from the webpage.

Way of Smoke Testing

Smoke Testing is usually done manually though there is a possibility of accomplishing the same through automation. It may vary from organization to organization.

Manual Smoke Testing

In general, smoke testing is done manually. It approaches varies from one organization to other. Smoke testing is carried to ensure the navigation of critical paths is as expected and doesn't hamper the functionality. Once the build is released to QA, high priority functionality test cases are to be taken and are tested to find the critical defects in the system. If the test passes, we continue the functional testing. If the test fails, the build is rejected and sent back to the development team for correction. QA again starts smoke testing with a new build version. Smoke testing is performed on new build and will get integrated with old builds to maintain the correctness of the system. Before performing smoke testing, QA team should check for correct build versions.

Smoke Testing by Automation

Automation Testing is used for Regression Testing. However, we can also use a set of automated test cases to run against Smoke Test. With the help of automation tests, developers can check build immediately, whenever there is a new build ready for deployment.

Instead of having repeated test manually whenever the new software build is deployed, recorded smoke test cases are executed against the build. It verifies whether the major functionalities still operates properly. If the test fails, then they can correct the build and redeploy the build immediately. By this, we can save time and ensure a quality build to the QA environment.

Using an automated tool, test engineer records all manual steps that are performed in the software build.

Smoke Testing Cycle

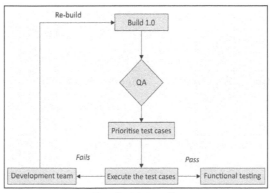

Smoke test cycle

Below flow chart shows how Smoke Testing is executed. Once the build is deployed in QA and, smoke tests are passed we proceed for functional testing. If the smoke test fails, we exit testing until the issue in the build is fixed.

Advantages of Smoke Testing

Here are few advantages listed for Smoke Testing:

- Easy to perform testing
- Defects will be identified in early stages
- Improves the quality of the system
- Reduces the risk
- Progress is easier to access
- Saves test effort and time
- Easy to detect critical errors and correction of errors
- It runs quickly
- Minimizes integration risks.

What Happens if we don't do Smoke Testing

If we don't perform smoke testing in early stages, defects may be encountered in later stages where it can be cost effective. And the Defect found in later stages can be show stoppers where it may affect the release of deliverables.

Sample smoke test cases example:

T.ID	Test scenarios	Description	Test step	Expected result	Actual result	Status
1	Valid login credentials	Test the login functionality of the web application to ensure that a registered user is allowed to log-in with username and password	1. Launch the application 2. Navigate the login page 3. Enter valid username 4. Enter valid password 5. Click on login button	Login should be success	As expected	Pass
2	Adding item func-tionality	Able to add item to the cart	1. Select categories list 2. Add the item to cart	Item should get added to the cart	Item is not getting added to the cart	Fail
3	Sign out function-ality	Check sign out functionality	1. select sign out button	The user should be able to sign out.	User is not able to sign out	

WHITE-BOX TESTING

White-box testing (also known as clear box testing, glass box testing, transparent box testing, and structural testing) is a method of software testing that tests internal structures or workings of an application, as opposed to its functionality (i.e. black-box testing). In white-box testing an internal perspective of the system, as well as programming skills, are used to design test cases. The tester chooses inputs to exercise paths through the code and determine the expected outputs. This is analogous to testing nodes in a circuit, e.g. in-circuit testing (ICT). White-box testing can be applied at the unit, integration and system levels of the software testing process. Although traditional testers tended to think of white-box testing as being done at the unit level, it is used for integration and system testing more frequently today. It can test paths within a unit, paths between units during integration, and between subsystems during a system–level test. Though this method of test design can uncover many errors or problems, it has the potential to miss unimplemented parts of the specification or missing requirements.

White-box test design techniques include the following code coverage criteria:

- Control flow testing
- Data flow testing
- Branch testing
- Statement coverage
- Decision coverage
- Modified condition/decision coverage
- Prime path testing
- Path testing.

White-box testing is a method of testing the application at the level of the source code. These test cases are derived through the use of the design techniques mentioned above: control flow testing, data flow testing, branch testing, path testing, statement coverage and decision coverage as well as modified condition/decision coverage. White-box testing is the use of these techniques as guidelines to create an error-free environment by examining any fragile code. These white-box testing techniques are the building blocks of white-box testing, whose essence is the careful testing of the application at the source code level to prevent any hidden errors later on. These different techniques exercise every visible path of the source code to minimize errors and create an error-free environment. The whole point of white-box testing is the ability to know which line of the code is being executed and being able to identify what the correct output should be.

Levels

1. Unit testing: White-box testing is done during unit testing to ensure that the code is working as intended; before any integration happens with previously tested code. White-box testing during unit testing catches any defects early on and aids in any defects that happen later on after the code is integrated with the rest of the application and therefore prevents any type of errors later on.

2. Integration testing: White-box testing at this level is written to test the interactions of interfaces with each other. The unit level testing made sure that each code was tested and working accordingly in an isolated environment and integration examines the correctness of the behaviour in an open environment through the use of white-box testing for any interactions of interfaces that are known to the programmer.

3. Regression testing: White-box testing during regression testing is the use of recycled white-box test cases at the unit and integration testing levels.

Basic Procedure

White-box testing's basic procedures require the tester to have an in-depth knowledge of the source code being tested. The programmer must have a deep understanding of the application to know what kinds of test cases to create so that every visible path is exercised for testing. Once the source code is understood then the source code can be analyzed for test cases to be created.

The following are the three basic steps that white-box testing takes in order to create test cases:

- Input involves different types of requirements, functional specifications, detailed designing of documents, proper source code and security specifications. This is the preparation stage of white-box testing to lay out all of the basic information.

- Processing involves performing risk analysis to guide whole testing process, proper test plan, execute test cases and communicate results. This is the phase of building test cases to make sure they thoroughly test the application the given results are recorded accordingly.

- Output involves preparing final report that encompasses all of the above preparations and results.

Advantages

White-box testing is one of the two biggest testing methods used today. It has several major advantages:

- Side effects of having the knowledge of the source code are beneficial to thorough testing.

- Optimization of code becomes easy as inconspicuous bottlenecks are exposed.

- Gives the programmer introspection because developers carefully describe any new implementation.

- Provides traceability of tests from the source, thereby allowing future changes to the source to be easily captured in the newly added or modified tests.

- Easy to automate.

- Provides clear, engineering-based rules for when to stop testing.

Disadvantages

Although white-box testing has great advantages, it is not perfect and contains some disadvantages:

- White-box testing brings complexity to testing because the tester must have knowledge of the program, or the test team needs to have at least one very good programmer who can understand the program at the code level. White-box testing requires a programmer with a high level of knowledge due to the complexity of the level of testing that needs to be done.

- On some occasions, it is not realistic to be able to test every single existing condition of the application and some conditions will be untested.

- The tests focus on the software as it exists, and missing functionality may not be discovered.

- The resulting test can be fragile because they are tightly coupled to the specific implementation of the thing being tested. The code under test could be rewritten to implement the same functionality in a different way that invalidates the assumptions baked into the test. This could result in tests that fail unnecessarily or, in the worst case, tests that now give false positives and mask errors in the code.

Modern View

A more modern view is that the dichotomy between white-box testing and black-box testing has blurred and is becoming less relevant. Whereas "white-box" originally meant using the source code, and black-box meant using requirements, tests are now derived from many documents at various levels of abstraction. The real point is that tests are usually designed from an abstract structure such as the input space, a graph, or logical predicates, and the question is what level of abstraction we derive that abstract structure from. That can be the source code, requirements, input space descriptions, or one of dozens of types of design models. Therefore, the "white-box / black-box" distinction is less important and the terms are less relevant.

Hacking

In penetration testing, white-box testing refers to a method where a white hat hacker has full knowledge of the system being attacked. The goal of a white-box penetration test is to simulate a malicious insider who has knowledge of and possibly basic credentials for the target system.

BLACK-BOX TESTING

Black-box testing is a method of software testing that examines the functionality of an application without peering into its internal structures or workings. This method of test can be applied virtually to every level of software testing: unit, integration, system and acceptance. It is sometimes referred to as specification-based testing.

Test Procedures

Specific knowledge of the application's code, internal structure and programming knowledge in general is not required. The tester is aware of *what* the software is supposed to do but is not aware of *how* it does it. For instance, the tester is aware that a particular input returns a certain, invariable output but is not aware of *how* the software produces the output in the first place.

Test Cases

Test cases are built around specifications and requirements, i.e., what the application is supposed to do. Test cases are generally derived from external descriptions of the software, including specifications, requirements and design parameters. Although the tests used are primarily *functional* in nature, *non-functional* tests may also be used. The test designer selects both valid and invalid inputs and determines the correct output, often with the help of a test oracle or a previous result that is known to be good, without any knowledge of the test object's internal structure.

Test Design Techniques

Typical black-box test design techniques include:

- Decision table testing
- All-pairs testing
- Equivalence partitioning
- Boundary value analysis
- Cause–effect graph
- Error guessing
- State transition testing
- Use case testing
- User story testing
- Domain analysis
- Syntax testing
- Combining technique.

Hacking

In penetration testing, black-box testing refers to a method where an ethical hacker has no knowledge of the system being attacked. The goal of a black-box penetration test is to simulate an external hacking or cyber warfare attack.

GRAY-BOX TESTING

Gray-box testing (International English spelling: grey-box testing) is a combination of white-box testing and black-box testing. The aim of this testing is to search for the defects if any due to improper structure or improper usage of applications.

A black-box tester is unaware of the internal structure of the application to be tested, while a white-box tester has access to the internal structure of the application. A gray-box tester partially knows the internal structure, which includes access to the documentation of internal data structures as well as the algorithms used. Gray-box testers require both high-level and detailed documents describing the application, which they collect in order to define test cases.

Need for Gray-box Testing

Gray-box testing is beneficial because it takes the straightforward technique of black-box testing and combines it with the code-targeted systems in white-box testing. Gray-box testing is based on requirement test case generation because it presents all the conditions before the program is tested by using the assertion method. A requirement specification language is used to make it easy to understand the requirements and verify its correctness.

Gray-box Testing Assumptions for Object-oriented Software

Object-oriented software consists primarily of objects; where objects are single indivisible units having executable code and/or data. Some assumptions are stated below which are needed for the application of use gray-box testing.

- Activation of Methods.
- State Reporting in Class Under Test (CUT).
- Report Testing is inherent in Class Under Test.

Examples

- Architectural model.
- Unified Modeling Language - UML Design Model.
- Finite-state machine - State Model.

Techniques

Cem Kaner defines "gray-box testing as involving inputs and outputs, but test design is educated by information about the code or the program operation of a kind that would normally be out of view of the tester". Gray-box testing techniques are:

- Matrix Testing: States the status report of the project.
- Regression testing: It implies rerunning of the test cases if new changes are made.
- Pattern Testing: Verify the good application for its design or architecture and patterns.
- Orthogonal array testing: used as subset of all possible combination.

Effects

Positive Effects

- Offers combined benefits: As Gray-box testing is combination of white-box and black-box testing, it serves advantages from both the testing's.

- Non-Intrusive: It is based on functional specification, architectural view whereas not on source code or binaries which makes it invasive too.

- Intelligent Test Authoring: Gray-box tester handles intelligent test scenario, for example, data type handling, communication protocol, exception handling.

- Unbiased Testing: In spite of all above advantages and functionalities, Gray-box testing maintains boundary for testing between tester and developer.

Negative Effects

- Partial code coverage: In gray-box testing, source code or binaries are missing because of limited access to internal or structure of the applications which results in limited access for code path traversal.

- Defect Identification: In distributed applications, it is difficult to associate defect identification. Still, Gray-box testing is a boon to find how appropriate these systems throw exceptions and how fine are these exceptions handled in distributed systems having web services environment.

Applications

- Gray-box testing is well suited for web applications. Web applications have distributed network or systems; due to absence of source code or binaries it is not possible to use white-box testing. Black-box testing is also not used due to just contract between customer and developer, so it is more efficient to use gray-box testing as significant information is available in Web Services Description Language (WSDL).

- Gray-box testing is suited for functional or business domain testing. Functional testing is done basically a test of user interactions with may be external systems. Gray-box testing is well-suited for functional testing due to its characteristics; it also helps to confirm that software meets the requirements defined for the software.

The distributed nature of Web services allows gray-box testing to detect defects within a service-oriented architecture (SOA). As we know, white-box testing is not suitable for Web services as it deals directly with the internal structures. White-box testing can be used for state art methods; for example, message mutation which generates the automatic tests for large arrays to help exception handling states, flow without source code or binaries. Such a strategy is useful to push gray-box testing nearer to the outcomes of white-box testing.

EXPLORATORY TESTING

Exploratory testing is an approach to software testing that is concisely described as simultaneous learning, test design and test execution. Cem Kaner, who coined the term in 1984, defines exploratory testing as "a style of software testing that emphasizes the personal freedom and responsibility of the individual tester to continually optimize the quality of his/her work by treating test-related learning, test design, test execution, and test result interpretation as mutually supportive activities that run in parallel throughout the project."

While the software is being tested, the tester learns things that together with experience and creativity generate new good tests to run. Exploratory testing is often thought of as a black box testing technique. Instead, those who have studied it consider it a test *approach* that can be applied to any test technique, at any stage in the development process. The key is not the test technique nor the item being tested or reviewed; the key is the cognitive engagement of the tester, and the tester's responsibility for managing his or her time.

Exploratory testing seeks to find out how the software actually works, and to ask questions about how it will handle difficult and easy cases. The quality of the testing is dependent on the tester's skill of inventing test cases and finding defects. The more the tester knows about the product and different test methods, the better the testing will be.

To further explain, comparison can be made of freestyle exploratory testing to its antithesis scripted testing. In the latter activity test cases are designed in advance. This includes both the individual steps and the expected results. These tests are later performed by a tester who compares the actual result with the expected. When performing exploratory testing, expectations are open. Some results may be predicted and expected; others may not. The tester configures, operates, observes, and evaluates the product and its behavior, critically investigating the result, and reporting information that seems likely to be a bug (which threatens the value of the product to some person) or an issue (which threatens the quality of the testing effort).

In reality, testing almost always is a combination of exploratory and scripted testing, but with a tendency towards either one, depending on context.

According to Kaner and James Marcus Bach, exploratory testing is more a mindset or "a way of thinking about testing" than a methodology. They also say that it crosses a continuum from slightly exploratory (slightly ambiguous or vaguely scripted testing) to highly exploratory (freestyle exploratory testing).

The documentation of exploratory testing ranges from documenting all tests performed to just documenting the bugs. During pair testing, two persons create test cases together; one performs them, and the other documents. Session-based testing is a method specifically designed to make exploratory testing auditable and measurable on a wider scale.

Exploratory testers often use tools, including screen capture or video tools as a record of the exploratory session, or tools to quickly help generate situations of interest, e.g. James Bach's Perlclip.

Benefits and Drawbacks

The main advantage of exploratory testing is that less preparation is needed, important bugs are found quickly, and at execution time, the approach tends to be more intellectually stimulating than execution of scripted tests.

Another major benefit is that testers can use deductive reasoning based on the results of previous results to guide their future testing on the fly. They do not have to complete a current series of scripted tests before focusing in on or moving on to exploring a more target rich environment. This also accelerates bug detection when used intelligently.

Another benefit is that, after initial testing, most bugs are discovered by some sort of exploratory testing. This can be demonstrated logically by stating, "Programs that pass certain tests tend to continue to pass the same tests and are more likely to fail other tests or scenarios that are yet to be explored."

Disadvantages are that tests invented and performed on the fly can't be reviewed in advance (and by that prevent errors in code and test cases), and that it can be difficult to show exactly which tests have been run.

Freestyle exploratory test ideas, when revisited, are unlikely to be performed in exactly the same manner, which can be an advantage if it is important to find new errors; or a disadvantage if it is more important to repeat specific details of the earlier tests. This can be controlled with specific instruction to the tester, or by preparing automated tests where feasible, appropriate, and necessary, and ideally as close to the unit level as possible.

Scientific Studies

Replicated experiment has shown that while scripted and exploratory testing result in similar defect detection effectiveness (the total number of defects found) exploratory results in higher efficiency (the number of defects per time unit) as no effort is spent on pre-designing the test cases. Observational study on exploratory testers proposed that the use of knowledge about the domain, the system under test, and customers is an important factor explaining the effectiveness of exploratory testing. A case-study of three companies found that ability to provide rapid feedback was a benefit of Exploratory Testing while managing test coverage was pointed as a short-coming. A survey found that Exploratory Testing is also used in critical domains and that Exploratory Testing approach places high demands on the person performing the testing.

Usage

Exploratory testing is particularly suitable if requirements and specifications are incomplete, or if there is lack of time. The approach can also be used to verify that previous testing has found the most important defects.

UNIT TESTING

In computer programming, unit testing is a software testing method by which individual units of source code, sets of one or more computer program modules together with associated control data, usage procedures, and operating procedures, are tested to determine whether they are fit for use.

Unit tests are typically automated tests written and run by software developers to ensure that a section of an application (known as the "unit") meets its design and behaves as intended. In procedural programming, a unit could be an entire module, but it is more commonly an individual function or procedure. In object-oriented programming, a unit is often an entire interface, such as a class, but could be an individual method. By writing tests first for the smallest testable units, then the compound behaviors between those, one can build up comprehensive tests for complex applications.

To isolate issues that may arise, each test case should be tested independently. Substitutes such as method stubs, mock objects, fakes, and test harnesses can be used to assist testing a module in isolation.

During development, a software developer may code criteria, or result that is known to be good, into the test to verify the unit's correctness. During test case execution, frameworks log tests that fail any criterion and report them in a summary.

Writing and maintaining unit tests can be made faster by using Parameterized Tests (PUTs). These allow the execution of one test multiple times with different input sets, thus reducing test code duplication. Unlike traditional unit tests, which are usually closed methods and test invariant conditions, PUTs take any set of parameters. PUTs have been supported by TestNG, JUnit and its .Net counterpart, XUnit. Suitable parameters for the unit tests may be supplied manually or in some cases are automatically generated by the test framework. In recent years support was added for writing more powerful (unit) tests, leveraging the concept of Theory. A parameterized test uses same execution steps with multiple input sets that are pre-defined. A theory is a test case that executes the same steps still, but inputs can be provided by a data generating method at run time.

Advantages

The goal of unit testing is to isolate each part of the program and show that the individual parts are correct. A unit test provides a strict, written contract that the piece of code must satisfy. As a result, it affords several benefits.

Unit testing finds problems early in the development cycle. This includes both bugs in the programmer's implementation and flaws or missing parts of the specification for the unit. The process of writing a thorough set of tests forces the author to think through inputs, outputs, and error conditions, and thus more crisply define the unit's desired behavior. The cost of finding a bug before coding begins or when the code is first written is considerably lower than the cost of detecting, identifying, and correcting the bug later. Bugs in released code may also cause costly problems for the end-users of the software. Code can be impossible or difficult to unit test if poorly written, thus unit testing can force developers to structure functions and objects in better ways.

In test-driven development (TDD), which is frequently used in both extreme programming and scrum, unit tests are created before the code itself is written. When the tests pass, that code is considered complete. The same unit tests are run against that function frequently as the larger code base is developed either as the code is changed or via an automated process with the build. If the unit tests fail, it is considered to be a bug either in the changed code or the tests themselves. The unit tests then allow the location of the fault or failure to be easily traced. Since the unit tests alert the development team of the problem before handing the code off to testers or clients, potential problems are caught early in the development process.

Unit testing allows the programmer to refactor code or upgrade system libraries at a later date, and make sure the module still works correctly (e.g., in regression testing). The procedure is to write test cases for all functions and methods so that whenever a change causes a fault, it can be quickly identified. Unit tests detect changes which may break a design contract.

Unit testing may reduce uncertainty in the units themselves and can be used in a bottom-up testing style approach. By testing the parts of a program first and then testing the sum of its parts, integration testing becomes much easier.

Unit testing provides a sort of living documentation of the system. Developers looking to learn what functionality is provided by a unit, and how to use it, can look at the unit tests to gain a basic understanding of the unit's interface (API).

Unit test cases embody characteristics that are critical to the success of the unit. These characteristics can indicate appropriate/inappropriate use of a unit as well as negative behaviors that are to be trapped by the unit. A unit test case, in and of itself, documents these critical characteristics, although many software development environments do not rely solely upon code to document the product in development.

When software is developed using a test-driven approach, the combination of writing the unit test to specify the interface plus the refactoring activities performed after the test has passed, may take the place of formal design. Each unit test can be seen as a design element specifying classes, methods, and observable behavior.

Limitations and Disadvantages

Testing will not catch every error in the program, because it cannot evaluate every execution path in any but the most trivial programs. This problem is a superset of the halting problem, which is undecidable. The same is true for unit testing. Additionally, unit testing by definition only tests the functionality of the units themselves. Therefore, it will not catch integration errors or broader system-level errors (such as functions performed across multiple units, or non-functional test areas such as performance). Unit testing should be done in conjunction with other software testing activities, as they can only show the presence or absence of particular errors; they cannot prove a complete absence of errors. To guarantee correct behavior for every execution path and every possible input, and ensure the absence of errors, other techniques are required, namely the application of formal methods to proving that a software component has no unexpected behavior.

An elaborate hierarchy of unit tests does not equal integration testing. Integration with peripheral units should be included in integration tests, but not in unit tests. Integration testing typically still relies heavily on humans testing manually; high-level or global-scope testing can be difficult to automate, such that manual testing often appears faster and cheaper.

Software testing is a combinatorial problem. For example, every Boolean decision statement requires at least two tests: one with an outcome of "true" and one with an outcome of "false". As a result, for every line of code written, programmers often need 3 to 5 lines of test code. This obviously takes time and its investment may not be worth the effort. There are problems that cannot easily be tested at all – for example those that are nondeterministic or involve multiple threads. In addition, code for a unit test is likely to be at least as buggy as the code it is testing.

Another challenge related to writing the unit tests is the difficulty of setting up realistic and useful tests. It is necessary to create relevant initial conditions so the part of the application being tested behaves like part of the complete system. If these initial conditions are not set correctly, the test will not be exercising the code in a realistic context, which diminishes the value and accuracy of unit test results.

To obtain the intended benefits from unit testing, rigorous discipline is needed throughout the software development process. It is essential to keep careful records not only of the tests that have been performed, but also of all changes that have been made to the source code of this or any other unit in the software. Use of a version control system is essential. If a later version of the unit fails a particular test that it had previously passed, the version-control software can provide a list of the source code changes (if any) that have been applied to the unit since that time.

It is also essential to implement a sustainable process for ensuring that test case failures are reviewed regularly and addressed immediately. If such a process is not implemented and ingrained into the team's workflow, the application will evolve out of sync with the unit test suite, increasing false positives and reducing the effectiveness of the test suite.

Unit testing embedded system software presents a unique challenge: Because the software is being developed on a different platform than the one it will eventually run on, you cannot readily run a test program in the actual deployment environment, as is possible with desktop programs.

Unit tests tend to be easiest when a method has input parameters and some output. It is not as easy to create unit tests when a major function of the method is to interact with something external to the application. For example, a method that will work with a database might require a mock up of database interactions to be created, which probably won't be as comprehensive as the real database interactions.

Example

Here is a set of test cases in Java that specify a number of elements of the implementation. First, that there must be an interface called Adder, and an implementing class with a zero-argument constructor called AdderImpl. It goes on to assert that the Adder interface should have a method called add, with two integer parameters, which returns another integer. It also specifies the behaviour of this method for a small range of values over a number of test methods.

```
import org.junit.Test;

public class TestAdder {

  @Test
  public void testSumPositiveNumbersOneAndOne() {
  Adder adder = new AdderImpl();
  assert(adder.add(1, 1) == 2);
  }

  // can it add the positive numbers 1 and 2?
  @Test
  public void testSumPositiveNumbersOneAndTwo() {
  Adder adder = new AdderImpl();
  assert(adder.add(1, 2) == 3);
  }

  // can it add the positive numbers 2 and 2?
```

```
@Test
public void testSumPositiveNumbersTwoAndTwo() {
Adder adder = new AdderImpl();
assert(adder.add(2, 2) == 4);
}

// is zero neutral?
@Test
public void testSumZeroNeutral() {
Adder adder = new AdderImpl();
assert(adder.add(0, 0) == 0);
}

// can it add the negative numbers -1 and -2?
@Test
public void testSumNegativeNumbers() {
Adder adder = new AdderImpl();
assert(adder.add(-1, -2) == -3);
}

// can it add a positive and a negative?
@Test
public void testSumPositiveAndNegative() {
Adder adder = new AdderImpl();
assert(adder.add(-1, 1) == 0);
}

// how about larger numbers?
@Test
public void testSumLargeNumbers() {
Adder adder = new AdderImpl();
assert(adder.add(1234, 988) == 2222);
}

}
```

In this case the unit tests, having been written first, act as a design document specifying the form and behaviour of a desired solution, but not the implementation details, which are left for the programmer. Following the "do the simplest thing that could possibly work" practice, the easiest solution that will make the test pass is shown below:

```
interface Adder {
 int add(int a, int b);
}
class AdderImpl implements Adder {
 public int add(int a, int b) {
 return a + b;
 }
}
```

As Executable Specifications

Using unit-tests as a design specification has one significant advantage over other design methods.

The design document (the unit-tests themselves) can itself be used to verify the implementation. The tests will never pass unless the developer implements a solution according to the design.

Unit testing lacks some of the accessibility of a diagrammatic specification such as a UML diagram, but they may be generated from the unit test using automated tools. Most modern languages have free tools (usually available as extensions to IDEs). Free tools, like those based on the xUnit framework, outsource to another system the graphical rendering of a view for human consumption.

Applications

Extreme Programming

Unit testing is the cornerstone of extreme programming, which relies on an automated unit testing framework. This automated unit testing framework can be either third party, e.g., xUnit, or created within the development group.

Extreme programming uses the creation of unit tests for test-driven development. The developer writes a unit test that exposes either a software requirement or a defect. This test will fail because either the requirement isn't implemented yet, or because it intentionally exposes a defect in the existing code. Then, the developer writes the simplest code to make the test, along with other tests, pass.

Most code in a system is unit tested, but not necessarily all paths through the code. Extreme programming mandates a "test everything that can possibly break" strategy, over the traditional "test every execution path" method. This leads developers to develop fewer tests than classical methods, but this isn't really a problem, more a restatement of fact, as classical methods have rarely ever been followed methodically enough for all execution paths to have been thoroughly tested. Extreme programming simply recognizes that testing is rarely exhaustive (because it is often too expensive and time-consuming to be economically viable) and provides guidance on how to effectively focus limited resources.

Crucially, the test code is considered a first class project artifact in that it is maintained at the same quality as the implementation code, with all duplication removed. Developers release unit testing code to the code repository in conjunction with the code it tests. Extreme programming's thorough unit testing allows the benefits mentioned above, such as simpler and more confident code development and refactoring, simplified code integration, accurate documentation, and more modular designs. These unit tests are also constantly run as a form of regression test.

Unit testing is also critical to the concept of Emergent Design. As emergent design is heavily dependent upon refactoring, unit tests are an integral component.

Unit Testing Frameworks

Unit testing frameworks are most often third-party products that are not distributed as part of the compiler suite. They help simplify the process of unit testing, having been developed for a wide variety of languages. Examples of testing frameworks include open source solutions such as the various code-driven testing frameworks known collectively as xUnit, and proprietary/commercial solutions such as Cantata for C/C++Typemock Isolator.NET/Isolator++, TBrun, JustMock, Parasoft Development Testing (Jtest, Parasoft C/C++test, dotTEST), Testwell CTA++ and Vector CAST/C++.

It is generally possible to perform unit testing without the support of a specific framework by writing client code that exercises the units under test and uses assertions, exception handling, or other control flow mechanisms to signal failure. Unit testing without a framework is valuable in that there is a barrier to entry for the adoption of unit testing; having scant unit tests is hardly better than having none at all, whereas once a framework is in place, adding unit tests becomes relatively easy. In some frameworks many advanced unit test features are missing or must be hand-coded.

Language-level Unit Testing Support

Some programming languages directly support unit testing. Their grammar allows the direct declaration of unit tests without importing a library (whether third party or standard). Additionally, the boolean conditions of the unit tests can be expressed in the same syntax as boolean expressions used in non-unit test code, such as what is used for if and while statements.

Languages with built-in unit testing support include:

- Apex

- Cobra

- Crystal

- D

- Go

- LabVIEW

- MATLAB

- Python

- Racket

- Ruby

- Rust

Some languages without built-in unit-testing support have very good unit testing libraries/frameworks. Those languages include:

- ABAP

- C#

- Clojure

- Elixir

- Java

- JavaScript

- Objective-C

- Perl

- PHP

- PowerShell

- Scala

- tcl

- Visual Basic .NET

- Xojo with XojoUnit.

INTEGRATION TESTING

Integration Testing is defined as a type of testing where software modules are integrated logically and tested as a group. A typical software project consists of multiple software modules, coded by different programmers. Integration Testing focuses on checking data communication amongst these modules.

Hence it is also termed as 'I & T' (Integration and Testing), 'String Testing' and sometimes 'Thread Testing'.

Need of Integration Testing

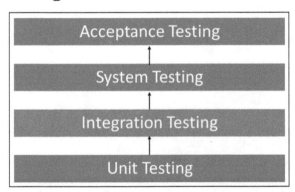

Although each software module is unit tested, defects still exist for various reasons like:

- A Module, in general, is designed by an individual software developer whose understanding and programming logic may differ from other programmers. Integration Testing becomes necessary to verify the software modules work in unity.

- At the time of module development, there are wide chances of change in requirements by the clients. These new requirements may not be unit tested and hence system integration Testing becomes necessary.

- Interfaces of the software modules with the database could be erroneous.

- External Hardware interfaces, if any, could be erroneous.

- Inadequate exception handling could cause issues.

Example of Integration Test Case

Integration Test Case differs from other test cases in the sense it focuses mainly on the interfaces & flow of data/information between the modules. Here priority is to be given for the integrating links rather than the unit functions which are already tested.

Sample Integration Test Cases for the following scenario: Application has 3 modules say 'Login Page', 'Mailbox' and 'Delete emails' and each of them is integrated logically. Here do not concentrate much on the Login Page testing as it's already been done in Unit Testing. But check how it's linked to the Mail Box Page.

Similarly Mail Box: Check its integration to the Delete Mails Module.

Test Case ID	Test Case Objective	Test Case Description	Expected Result
1	Check the interface link between the Login and Mailbox module	Enter login credentials and click on the Login button	To be directed to the Mail Box
2	Check the interface link between the Mailbox and Delete Mails Module	From Mailbox select the email and click a delete button	Selected email should appear in the Deleted/Trash folder

Strategies of Integration Testing

Software Engineering defines variety of strategies to execute Integration testing, viz.

- Big Bang Approach

- Incremental Approach which is further divided into the following:

  ○ Top Down Approach

  ○ Bottom Up Approach

  ○ Sandwich Approach - Combination of Top Down and Bottom Up.

Below are the different strategies, the way they are executed and their limitations as well advantages.

Big Bang Approach

Here all component are integrated together at once and then tested.

Advantages:

- Convenient for small systems.

Disadvantages:

- Fault Localization is difficult.

- Given the sheer number of interfaces that need to be tested in this approach, some interfaces link to be tested could be missed easily.

- Since the Integration testing can commence only after "all" the modules are designed, the testing team will have less time for execution in the testing phase.

- Since all modules are tested at once, high-risk critical modules are not isolated and tested on priority. Peripheral modules which deal with user interfaces are also not isolated and tested on priority.

Incremental Approach

In this approach, testing is done by joining two or more modules that are *logically related*. Then the other related modules are added and tested for the proper functioning. The process continues until all of the modules are joined and tested successfully.

Incremental Approach, in turn, is carried out by two different Methods:

- Bottom Up
- Top Down

What is Stub and Driver?

Incremental Approach is carried out by using dummy programs called Stubs and Drivers. Stubs and Drivers do not implement the entire programming logic of the software module but just simulate data communication with the calling module.

Bottom-up Integration

In the bottom-up strategy, each module at lower levels is tested with higher modules until all modules are tested. It takes help of Drivers for testing.

Diagrammatic Representation

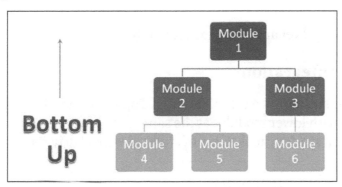

Advantages:

- Fault localization is easier.
- No time is wasted waiting for all modules to be developed unlike Big-bang approach.

Disadvantages:

- Critical modules (at the top level of software architecture) which control the flow of application are tested last and may be prone to defects.
- An early prototype is not possible.

Top-down Integration

In Top to down approach, testing takes place from top to down following the control flow of the software system.

Diagrammatic Representation

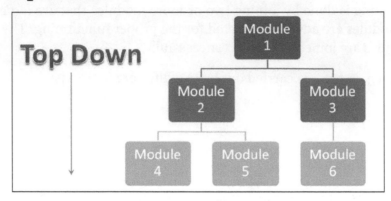

Advantages:

- Fault Localization is easier.

- Possibility to obtain an early prototype.

- Critical Modules are tested on priority; major design flaws could be found and fixed first.

Disadvantages:

- Needs many Stubs.

- Modules at a lower level are tested inadequately.

Hybrid/Sandwich Integration

In the sandwich/hybrid strategy is a combination of Top Down and Bottom up approaches. Here, top modules are tested with lower modules at the same time lower modules are integrated with top modules and tested. This strategy makes use of stubs as well as drivers.

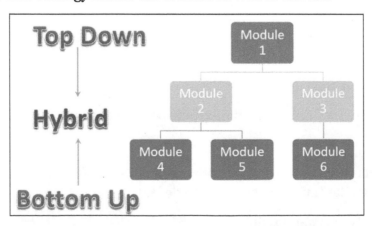

How to do Integration Testing?

The Integration test procedure irrespective of the Software testing strategies (discussed above):

1. Prepare the Integration Tests Plan.

2. Design the Test Scenarios, Cases, and Scripts.

3. Executing the test Cases followed by reporting the defects.

4. Tracking & re-testing the defects.

5. Steps 3 and 4 are repeated until the completion of Integration is successful.

Integration Test Plans

It includes the following attributes:

- Methods/Approaches to testing.

- Scopes and Out of Scopes Items of Integration Testing.

- Roles and Responsibilities.

- Pre-requisites for Integration testing.

- Testing environment.

- Risk and Mitigation Plans.

Entry and Exit Criteria of Integration Testing

Entry and Exit Criteria to Integration testing phase in any software development model.

Entry Criteria:

- Unit Tested Components/Modules.

- All High prioritized bugs fixed and closed.

- All Modules to be code completed and integrated successfully.

- Integration tests Plan, test case, scenarios to be signed off and documented.

- Required Test Environment to be set up for Integration testing.

Exit Criteria:

- Successful Testing of Integrated Application.

- Executed Test Cases are documented.

- All High prioritized bugs fixed and closed.

- Technical documents to be submitted followed by release Notes.

Best Practices/Guidelines for Integration Testing:

- First, determine the Integration Test Strategy that could be adopted and later prepare the test cases and test data accordingly.

- Study the Architecture design of the Application and identify the Critical Modules. These need to be tested on priority.

- Obtain the interface designs from the Architectural team and create test cases to verify all of the interfaces in detail. Interface to database/external hardware/software application must be tested in detail.

- After the test cases, it's the test data which plays the critical role.

- Always have the mock data prepared, prior to executing. Do not select test data while executing the test cases.

COMPATIBILITY TESTING

Compatibility testing is a non-functional testing technique, which is generally performed to validate and verify the compatibility of the developed software product or website with various other objects, such as other web browsers, hardware platforms, users, operating systems, etc. Performed during the early stages of quality assurance, compatibility testing enables the team to ensure that the compatibility requirements, requested by the client, are fulfilled and inbuilt in the end product.

Furthermore, compatibility testing enables the team to deliver a software product that works seamlessly across various configurations of the software's computing environments and offers consistent experience and performance across all platforms and to all users.

Categories of Compatibility Testing

Compatibility testing is a type of testing that allows software to work appropriately across and with various devices and platforms, which further helps the team to deliver a software that offers impeccable performance and user experience. Moreover, this type of testing can be categorized into 8 different categories, which are mentioned below:

- Hardware Compatibility Testing: The hardware compatibility testing validates the compatibility of the software with various other hardware configurations and ensures its accuracy.

- Operating System Compatibility Testing: During this type of compatibility testing, the software compatibility is tested with different operating systems, such as Mac OS X, Windows, UNIX, etc.

- Software Compatibility Testing: This type of testing is implemented to check the compatibility of the software with different software.

- Network Compatibility Testing: While performing network compatibility test, the team evaluates the performance of a system in a network with varying parameters, such as bandwidth, operating speed, capacity, etc. Additionally, it verifies the application in different networks with the assistance of these parameters.

- Browser Compatibility Testing: In this type of testing, the team verifies whether the built software or website is compatible and works properly with various browsers like IE, Google Chrome, Mozilla Firefox, etc.

- Devices Compatibility Testing: This is done to check the software's compatibility with different devices such as printers, scanners, bluetooth, and USBs.

- Mobile Compatibility Testing: Mobile compatibility test checks the compatibility of the software product with various mobile devices of different operating systems and sizes, such as iOS, Android and more.

- Software Version Testing: With the assistance of version compatibility test, the team verifies whether the software application is compatible with different versions of the software. This is further ensured through two of compatibility testing.

Types of Compatibility Testing

To ensure the compatibility of the built software product with various versions and platforms, two types of compatibility testing is used by the team of testers- backward compatibility testing and forward compatibility testing.

1. Backward Compatibility Testing: During the process of backward compatibility testing, the team verifies if the developed software or hardware product is compatible with older platforms or not. This type of testing is also known as downward compatible and is more predictable than forward compatibility testing, as all the dynamics of the potentially compatible platforms are known to the team in this case of testing.

2. Forward Compatibility Testing: Forward compatibility testing or forward compatible is a process of verifying and testing the developed software or hardware to ensure whether it is compatible with future versions of other platforms or not. However, forward compatibility testing is harder to execute than backward compatibility testing, as all the dynamics are not always known to the team members in this type of testing.

General Process for Compatibility Testing

The process of compatibility testing is an easy one and can be executed manually or with the assistance of numerous compatibility testing tools available in the industry. This process involves four important stages, which are:

Platform/Environment Identification: The initial step of the process is to identify and define the set of platform and environments that the application has to work on.

1. Design Test Cases & Configuration: During this stage of the process, different test cases and configurations are designed by the team. The testers performing this task should be experienced and must have in-depth knowledge of various platforms, versions, hardware, etc., to understand the workings of the application under various configurations.

2. Establish Test Cases & Environment: After designing the necessary test cases, the team works together to establish the environment for testing, wherein the compatibility of the software will be tested and verified.

3. Results Analysis & Reporting: Finally, the test is executed and the results are analyzed. Any defect, issue, bug, or discrepancies noticed by the team during this phase is recorded and reported to the responsible individual for rectification.

4. Rectification & Retesting: During this last stage of the process, the responsible team rectifies and resolves the issue and retests the software, to validate the accuracy of the process.

Reasons for Compatibility Testing

Nowadays, when software products are being developed in abundance, it is important for them to be perfect and effective to garner the attention of the users as well as the IT industry. Therefore, reasons for compatibility testing are numerous and without implementing it during software testing life cycle it is difficult to guarantee the compatibility as well as the performance and functionality of the software. Therefore, following are some of the reasons for performing compatibility testing:

- The main reason for compatibility testing is to ensure that the software is able to work without any issues on all devices and platforms.

- It ensures that the software product meets the specified requirements accurately.

- Helps improve the quality of the product.

- Offer remarkable user experience and helps increase opportunities for the organization.

Common Compatibility Testing Defects

During the process of compatibility testing, the team encounters a variety issues and defects, which become a major hurdle in providing remarkable and effective software compatibility. Hence, here is a list of defects and issues majorly encountered by the team, while performing compatibility testing:

- Modifications or changes in the user interface (UI), such as its look or feel.

- Any changes in the font size.

- Issues related to alignment can hamper the effectiveness as well as compatibility of the software.

- Changes in the CSS style and color.

- Any broken or incomplete tables or frames in the software can cause issues with its compatibility.

- Defects or issues in or related to the scroll bar.

Benefits of Compatibility Testing

Compatibility testing is an important testing process that offers numerous advantages and benefits to the testers, some of which are mentioned below:

- It helps to detect errors in the software product before it is delivered to the end users.

- Reduces the future help desk cost, which is mainly incurred for providing relevant and required customer support for various compatibility issues.

- Improves the process of software development, as it tackles all compatibility related issues and validates the performance and functionality of the software across various platforms and devices.

- Helps test the product's scalability, stability, and usability.

- With the assistance of compatibility testing, the team can validate that the software meets the business and user requirements and is optimized for quality.

- Ensures there is no loss of business if a potential customer visits an organization on any platform.

- Validates optimum user experience and 100% customer satisfaction.

Compatibility Testing Tools

When it comes to executing the process of compatibility testing, there are multifarious tools available in the market that can be utilized by the team of testers to validate the compatibility of the software. Some of the most popular tools used by testers worldwide for compatibility testing are:

- Browser Stack

- Browser Shots

- Virtual Desktop

- Secure Platform

- Cross Browser Testing

- Spoon Browser Sandbox

- IE Tab

- Equafy

- Testing Bot

- Browse Em All

- Adobe Browserlab

- Ghost Lab

- Browser Seal

- Microsoft Super Preview

- Simulator and Emulator.

REGRESSION TESTING

Regression testing (rarely *non-regression testing*) is re-running functional and non-functional tests to ensure that previously developed and tested software still performs after a change. If not, that would be called a *regression*. Changes that may require regression testing include bug fixes, software enhancements, configuration changes, and even substitution of electronic components. As regression test suites tend to grow with each found defect, test automation is frequently involved. Sometimes a change impact analysis is performed to determine an appropriate subset of tests (*non-regression analysis*).

As software is updated or changed, or reused on a modified target, emergence of new faults and/or re-emergence of old faults is quite common. Sometimes re-emergence occurs because a fix gets lost through poor revision control practices (or simple human error in revision control). Often, a fix for a problem will be "fragile" in that it fixes the problem in the narrow case where it was first observed but not in more general cases which may arise over the lifetime of the software. Frequently, a fix for a problem in one area inadvertently causes a software bug in another area. Finally, it may happen that, when some feature is redesigned, some of the same mistakes that were made in the original implementation of the feature are made in the redesign.

Therefore, in most software development situations, it is considered good coding practice, when a bug is located and fixed, to record a test that exposes the bug and re-run that test regularly after subsequent changes to the program. Although this may be done through manual testing procedures using programming techniques, it is often done using automated testing tools. Such a test suite contains software tools that allow the testing environment to execute all the regression test cases automatically; some projects even set up automated systems to re-run all regression tests at specified intervals and report any failures (which could imply a regression or an out-of-date test). Common strategies are to run such a system after every successful compile (for small projects), every night, or once a week. Those strategies can be automated by an external tool.

Regression testing is an integral part of the extreme programming software development method. In this method, design documents are replaced by extensive, repeatable, and automated testing of the entire software package throughout each stage of the software development process. Regression testing is done after functional testing has concluded, to verify that the other functionalities are working.

In the corporate world, regression testing has traditionally been performed by a software quality assurance team after the development team has completed work. However, defects found at this stage are the most costly to fix. This problem is being addressed by the rise of unit testing. Although developers have always written test cases as part of the development cycle, these test cases have generally been either functional tests or unit tests that verify only intended outcomes. Developer testing compels a developer to focus on unit testing and to include both positive and negative test cases.

Techniques

The various regression testing techniques are:

Retest All

This technique checks all the test cases on the current program to check its integrity. Though it is expensive as it needs to re-run all the cases, it ensures that there are no errors because of the modified code.

Regression Test Selection

Unlike Retest all, this technique runs a part of the test suite (owing to the cost of retest all) if the cost of selecting the part of the test suite is less than the Retest all technique.

Test Case Prioritization

Prioritize the test cases so as to increase a test suite's rate of fault detection. Test case prioritization techniques schedule test cases so that the test cases that are higher in priority are executed before the test cases that have a lower priority.

Types of Test Case Prioritization

- General prioritization – Prioritize test cases that will be beneficial on subsequent versions

- Version-specific prioritization – Prioritize test cases with respect to a particular version of the software.

Hybrid

This technique is a hybrid of regression test selection and test case prioritization.

Benefits and Drawbacks

Regression testing is performed when changes are made to the existing functionality of the software or if there is a bug fix in the software. Regression testing can be achieved through multiple approaches, if a *test all* approach is followed; it provides certainty that the changes made to the software have not affected the existing functionalities, which are unaltered.

In agile software development—where the software development life cycles are very short, resources are scarce, and changes to the software are very frequent—regression testing might introduce a lot of unnecessary overhead.

In a software development environment which tends to use black box components from a third party, performing regression testing can be tricky, as any change in the third-party component may interfere with the rest of the system (and performing regression testing on a third-party component is difficult, because it is an unknown entity).

Uses

Regression testing can be used not only for testing the *correctness* of a program but often also for tracking the quality of its output. For instance, in the design of a compiler, regression testing could track the code size and the time it takes to compile and execute the test suite cases.

Also as a consequence of the introduction of new bugs, program maintenance requires far more system testing per statement written than any other programming. Theoretically, after each fix, one must run the entire batch of test cases previously run against the system to ensure that it has not been damaged in an obscure way. In practice, such *regression testing* must indeed approximate this theoretical idea, and it is very costly.

Regression tests can be broadly categorized as functional tests or unit tests. Functional tests exercise the complete program with various inputs. Unit tests exercise individual functions, subroutines, or object methods. Both functional testing tools and unit-testing tools tend to be automated and are often third-party products that are not part of the compiler suite. A functional test may be a scripted series of program inputs, possibly even involving an automated mechanism for controlling mouse movements and clicks. A unit test may be a set of separate functions within the code itself or a driver layer that links to the code without altering the code being tested.

CONTINUOUS TESTING

Continuous testing was originally proposed as a way of reducing waiting time for feedback to developers by introducing development environment-triggered tests as well as more traditional developer/tester-triggered tests. Continuous testing is the process of executing automated tests as part of the software delivery pipeline to obtain immediate feedback on the business risks associated with a software release candidate.

For Continuous testing, the scope of testing extends from validating bottom-up requirements or user stories to assessing the system requirements associated with overarching business goals.

Adoption Drivers

In the 2010s, software has become a key business differentiator. As a result, organizations now expect software development teams to deliver more, and more innovative, software within shorter delivery cycles. To meet these demands, teams have turned to lean approaches, such as Agile, DevOps, and Continuous Delivery, to try to speed up the SDLC. After accelerating other aspects of the delivery pipeline, teams typically find that their testing process is preventing them from achieving the expected benefits of their SDLC acceleration initiative. Testing and the overall quality process remain problematic for several key reasons.

- Traditional testing processes are too slow. Iteration length has changed from months to weeks or days with the rising popularity of Agile, DevOps, and Continuous Delivery. Traditional methods of testing, which rely heavily on manual testing and automated GUI tests that require frequent updating, cannot keep pace. At this point, organizations tend to recognize the need to extend their test automation efforts.

- Even after more automation is added to the existing test process, managers still lack adequate insight into the level of risk associated with an application at any given point in time. Understanding these risks is critical for making the rapid go/no go decisions involved in Continuous Delivery processes. If tests are developed without an understanding of what the business considers to be an acceptable level of risk, it is possible to have a release candidate that passes all the available tests, but which the business leaders would not consider to be ready for release. For the test results to accurately indicate whether each release candidate meets business expectations, the approach to designing tests must be based on the business's tolerance for risks related to security, performance, reliability, and compliance. In addition to having unit tests that check code at a very granular bottom-up level, there is a need for a broader suite of tests to provide a top-down assessment of the release candidate's business risk.

- Even if testing is automated and tests effectively measure the level of business risk, teams without a coordinated end-to-end quality process tend to have trouble satisfying the business expectations within today's compressed delivery cycles. Trying to remove risks at the end of each iteration has been shown to be significantly slower and more resource-intensive than building quality into the product through defect prevention strategies such as development testing.

Organizations adopt Continuous Testing because they recognize that these problems are preventing them from delivering quality software at the desired speed. They recognize the growing importance of software as well as the rising cost of software failure, and they are no longer willing to make a tradeoff between time, scope, and quality.

Goals and Benefits

The goal of continuous testing is to provide fast and continuous feedback regarding the level of business risk in the latest build or release candidate. This information can then be used to determine if the software is ready to progress through the delivery pipeline at any given time.

Since testing begins early and is executed continuously, application risks are exposed soon after they are introduced. Development teams can then prevent those problems from progressing to the next stage of the SDLC. This reduces the time and effort that need to be spent finding and fixing defects. As a result, it is possible to increase the speed and frequency at which quality software (software that meets expectations for an acceptable level of risk) is delivered, as well as decrease technical debt.

Moreover, when software quality efforts and testing are aligned with business expectations, test execution produces a prioritized list of actionable tasks. This helps teams focus their efforts on the quality tasks that will have the greatest impact, based on their organization's goals and priorities.

Additionally, when teams are continuously executing a broad set of continuous tests throughout the SDLC, they amass metrics regarding the quality of the process as well as the state of the software. The resulting metrics can be used to re-examine and optimize the process itself, including the effectiveness of those tests. This information can be used to establish a feedback loop that helps teams incrementally improve the process. Frequent measurement, tight feedback loops, and continuous improvement are key principles of DevOps.

Scope of Testing

Continuous testing includes the validation of both functional requirements and non-functional requirements.

For testing functional requirements (functional testing), Continuous Testing often involves unit tests, API testing, integration testing, and system testing. For testing non-functional requirements (non-functional testing - to determine if the application meets expectations around performance, security, compliance, etc.), it involves practices such as static code analysis, security testing, performance testing, etc. Tests should be designed to provide the earliest possible detection (or prevention) of the risks that are most critical for the business or organization that is releasing the software.

Teams often find that in order to ensure that test suite can run continuously and effectively assesses the level of risk, it's necessary to shift focus from GUI testing to API testing because 1) APIs (the "transaction layer") are considered the most stable interface to the system under test, and 2) GUI tests require considerable rework to keep pace with the frequent changes typical of accelerated release processes; tests at the API layer are less brittle and easier to maintain.

Tests are executed during or alongside continuous integration—at least daily. For teams practicing continuous delivery, tests are commonly executed many times a day, every time that the application is updated in to the version control system.

Ideally, all tests are executed across all non-production test environments. To ensure accuracy and consistency, testing should be performed in the most complete, production-like environment possible. Strategies for increasing test environment stability include virtualization software (for dependencies your organization can control and image) service virtualization (for dependencies beyond your scope of control or unsuitable for imaging), and test data management.

Common Practices

- Testing should be a collaboration of Development, QA, and Operations—aligned with the priorities of the line of business—within a coordinated, end-to-end quality process.

- Tests should be logically-componentized, incremental, and repeatable; results must be deterministic and meaningful.

- All tests need to be run at some point in the build pipeline, but not all tests need be run all the time.

- Eliminate test data and environment constraints so that tests can run constantly and consistently in production-like environments.

- To minimize false positives, minimize test maintenance, and more effectively validate use cases across modern systems with multitier architectures, teams should emphasize API testing over GUI testing.

Challenges/Roadblocks

Since modern applications are highly distributed, test suites that exercise them typically require access to a dependencies that are not readily available for testing (e.g., third-party services, mainframes that are available for testing only in limited capacity or at inconvenient times, etc.) Moreover, with the growing adoption of Agile and parallel development processes, it is common for end-to-end functional tests to require access to dependencies that are still evolving or not yet implemented. This problem can be addressed by using service virtualization to simulate the application under test's (AUT's) interactions with the missing or unavailable dependencies. It can also be used to ensure that data, performance, and behavior is consistent across the various test runs.

One reason teams avoid continuous testing is that their infrastructure is not scalable enough to continuously execute the test suite. This problem can be addressed by focusing the tests on the business's priorities, splitting the test base, and parallelizing the testing with application release automation tools.

Continuous Testing vs. Automated Testing

The goal of Continuous Testing is to apply "extreme automation" to stable, production-like test environments. Automation is essential for Continuous Testing. But automated testing is not the same as Continuous Testing.

Automated testing involves automated, CI-driven execution of whatever set of tests the team has accumulated. Moving from automated testing to continuous testing involves executing a set of tests that is specifically designed to assess the business risks associated with a release candidate, and to regularly execute these tests in the context of stable, production-like test environments.

Some differences between automated and continuous testing:

- With automated testing, a test failure may indicate anything from a critical issue to a violation of a trivial naming standard. With continuous testing, a test failure always indicates a critical business risk.

- With continuous testing, a test failure is addressed via a clear workflow for prioritizing defects vs. business risks and addressing the most critical ones first.

- With continuous testing, each time a risk is identified, there is a process for exposing all similar defects that might already have been introduced, as well as preventing this same problem from recurring in the future.

Predecessors

Since the 1990s, Continuous test-driven development has been used to provide programmers rapid feedback on whether the code they added a) functioned properly and b) unintentionally changed or broke existing functionality. This testing, which was a key component of Extreme Programming, involves automatically executing unit tests (and sometimes acceptance tests or smoke tests) as part of the automated build, often many times a day. These tests are written prior to implementation; passing tests indicate that implementation is successful.

Continuous Testing Tools

In 2016, both Forrester Research and Gartner made Continuous Testing a primary consideration in their annual evaluations of test automation tools.

Gartner evaluated 9 tools that met their criteria for enterprise-grade test automation tools. The evaluation involved inquiries with Gartner clients, surveys of tool users, vendor responses to Gartner questions, vendor product demonstrations. Gartner required tools to support native Windows desktop application testing and Android or iOS testing support as well as support 3 of the following: responsive web applications, mobile applications, package applications, API/web services. The results of the 2016 Magic Quadrant research are:

- Leaders: Hewlett Packard Enterprise, Tricentis, IBM

- Challengers: Microsoft, Worksoft

- Visionaries: TestPlant, Micro Focus, SmartBear Software

- Niche players: Ranorex.

Forrester Research evaluated 11 tools that met their criteria for enterprise-grade test functional automation tools. Forrester determined 33 criteria based on past research, user needs, and expert interviews, then evaluated products versus those criteria based on vendor responses to Forrester questions, vendor product demonstrations, and customer interviews. Forrester required tools to have cross-browser, mobile, UI, and API testing capabilities. The results of the 2016 Forrester wave are:

- Leaders: Parasoft, IBM, Tricentis, Hewlett Packard Enterprise

- Strong performers: Microsoft, Micro Focus, SmartBear Software, TestPlant

- Contenders: Conformiq, Original Software, LogiGear.

SYSTEM TESTING

System testing is testing conducted on a complete integrated system to evaluate the system's compliance with its specified requirements.

System testing takes, as its input, all of the integrated components that have passed integration testing. The purpose of integration testing is to detect any inconsistencies between the units that are integrated together (called *assemblages*). System testing seeks to detect defects both within the "inter-assemblages" and also within the system as a whole. The actual result is the behavior produced or observed when a component or system is tested.

System testing is performed on the entire system in the context of either functional requirement specifications (FRS) or system requirement specification (SRS), or both. System testing tests not only the design, but also the behaviour and even the believed expectations of the customer. It is also intended to test up to and beyond the bounds defined in the software or hardware requirements specification(s).

Approaches

- Destructive testing: Tests are carried out to the specimen's failure, in order to understand a specimen's performance or material behaviour under different loads.

- Nondestructive testing: Analysis techniques to evaluate the properties of a material, component or system without causing damage.

Subject-specific Test Methods

Software Testing

Software testing is an investigation conducted to provide stakeholders with information about the quality of the software product or service under test. Software testing can also provide an objective, independent view of the software to allow the business to appreciate and understand the risks of software implementation. Software testing involves the execution of a software component or system component to evaluate one or more properties of interest. In general, these properties indicate the extent to which the component or system under test meets the requirements that guided its design and development, responds correctly to all kinds of inputs, performs its functions within an acceptable time, is sufficiently usable, can be installed and run in its intended environments, and achieves the general result its stakeholders desire. As the number of possible tests for even simple software components is practically infinite, all software testing uses some strategy to select tests that are feasible for the available time and resources.

Mobile-device Testing

Mobile-device testing assures the quality of mobile devices, like mobile phones, PDAs, etc. The testing will be conducted on both hardware and software. And from the view of different procedures, the testing comprises R&D testing, factory testing and certificate testing. Mobile-device testing involves a set of activities from monitoring and troubleshooting mobile application, content and services on real handsets. Testing includes verification and validation of hardware devices and software applications.

Destructive Testing

Destructive Testing is defined as a software testing type to find points of failure in a software program. It is a testing method where an application is intentionally made to fail to check the robustness of the application and identify the point of failure. Unlike other testing method which checks the function of an application, this technique will check the unpredictable user behavior within the application.

For Destructive Testing, it is not necessary to have the knowledge of the original requirements of a software product. However, some knowledge could help in developing a good testing strategy.

Why to do Destructive Testing

- It helps to understand predictable software behavior when the software is put under improper usage.

- It helps to check the robustness of a software product.

What you Check in Destructive Testing

In Destructive Testing, you will check for following things:

- Proper software behavior

- Improper software behavior

- Improper usage

- Improper input data

- Proper output data.

How to do Destructive Testing

Destructive Testing involves many activities like designing a set of test scripts, executing test scripts, raising bugs, closing bugs, and providing the pass or fail metrics to stakeholders at the end of the iteration.

For Destructive Testing, there are numerous ways it can be tested:

- Failure point analysis method: It is a walkthrough of the system conducting an assessment of what could go wrong at various points. For this strategy, help from BA (Business Analyst) may be taken.

- Tester peer review: Get your test cases analyzed or reviewed by a fellow tester, who is less familiar with the system/function.

- Business review of test cases: The end users or experts may think of many valid scenarios which sometimes testers may not have considered or missed as their entire focus will be on testing the requirements.

- Conduct exploratory testing, using run sheets: Exploratory testing using run sheets will help to determine what was tested, repeat the tests and allows you to control your test coverage.

- Use other source: You can ask someone to break the software product and analyze for various scenarios.

Destructive Testing Methods and Techniques

In Software Engineering, Destructive Testing method can use many testing techniques like:

- Alpha/Beta Testing

- Regression Testing

- Interface Testing

- Equivalence Partitioning

- Loop Testing

- Acceptance Testing, and so on.

While few techniques that can be used with modifications are, White Box Testing, Security Testing, Defect Testing, Smoke Testing, and so on.

While performing Destructive Testing, there are certain testing conditions:

- The software shall never process or accept invalid input data.

- Regardless of the validity or correctness of input data, the software should always produce proper output data.

Non Destructive Testing

Non destructive testing is defined as a software assessment method that involves interacting with the software correctly. In other words, NDT (Non destructive testing) can also be called as positive testing or "happy path" testing.

It gives the expected results and proves that the software is behaving as expected.

Example: Entering the correct data in a login module and checking whether it accepts credentials and navigates.

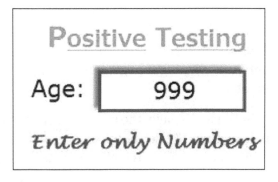

Need of Non Destructive Testing

- The major benefit of Non destructive testing is that it results in improved quality of software and bugs get fixed.

- To demonstrate that software functions are working according to the specification.

- The verify performance requirement has been met.

- To verify that the requirements of end users are met.

- To check the small section of code or functionality is working as expected and not breaking the related functionality.

- It is also the first form of testing that a tester would perform on an application.(i.e., at the initial stage of SDLC).

- Non destructive testing is usually done when we do not have enough time for testing.

Test Strategy for Non Destructive Testing

- Approach to Non destructive testing should be positive.

- The intention of testing is to prove that an application will work on giving valid input data.

- There is no special requirement to perform Non destructive testing.

- Best practice for Non destructive testing is to check whether the system does, what it is supposed to do.

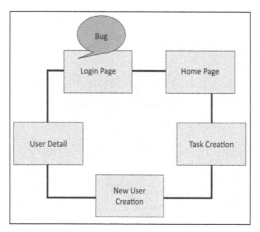

Example:

- An application has 5 modules viz, login page, home page, user detail page, new user creation and task creation, etc.

- Suppose we have a bug in the login page, the username field accepts less than six alpha-numeric characters. This is against the set requirements which state that username should not accept less than six characters. So in the above scenario, it is a bug.

- Now the bug is reported to the development team, and it is fixed and again sent back to the testing team. The testing team not only checks the login page where the defect is fixed but also tests the other modules as well. While testing all the modules, it performs the Non-destructive type of testing, just to check the whole application is working properly.

ACCEPTANCE TESTING

Once the System Testing process is completed by the testing team and is signed-off, the entire Product/application is handed over to the customer/few users of customers/both, to test for its acceptability i.e., Product/application should be flawless in meeting both the critical and major Business requirements. Also, end-to-end business flows are verified similar as in real-time scenario.

The production-like environment will be the testing environment for Accepting Testing (Usually termed as Staging, Pre-Prod, Fail-Over, UAT environment).

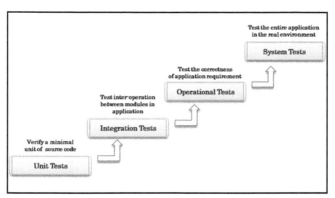

This is a black-box testing technique where only the functionality is verified to ensure that the product meets the specified acceptance criteria (no need for design/implementation knowledge).

Why Acceptance Tests?

Though System testing has been completed successfully, the Acceptance test is demanded by the customer. Tests conducted here are repetitive, as they would have been covered in System testing.

Then, why is this Testing is Conducted by Customers?

This is because:

- To gain confidence in the product that is getting released to the market.

- To ensure that the product is working in the way it has to.

- To ensure that the product matches current market standards and is competitive enough with the other similar products in the market.

Types

There are several types of this testing.

Few of them are listed below:

User Acceptance Testing (UAT)

UAT is to assess whether the Product is working for the user, correctly for the usage. Specific requirements which are quite often used by the end-users are primarily picked for the testing purpose. This is also termed as End-User Testing.

The term "User" here signifies the end-users to whom the Product/application is intended and hence, testing is performed from the end-users perspective and from their point of view.

Business Acceptance Testing (BAT)

This is to assess whether the Product meets the business goals and purposes or not.

BAT mainly focuses on business benefits (finances) which are quite challenging due to the changing market conditions/advancing technologies so that the current implementation may have to undergo changes which result in extra budgets.

Even the Product passing the technical requirements may fail BAT due to these reasons.

Contract Acceptance Testing (CAT)

This is a contract which specifies that once the Product goes live, within a predetermined period, the acceptance test must be performed and it should pass all the acceptance use cases.

Contract signed here is termed as Service Level Agreement (SLA), which includes the terms where the payment will be made only if the Product services are in-line with all the requirements, which means the contract is fulfilled.

Sometimes, this contract may happen before the Product goes live. Either the ways, a contract should be well defined in terms of the period of testing, areas of testing, conditions on issues encountered at later stages, payments, etc.

Regulations/Compliance Acceptance Testing (RAT)

This is to assess whether the Product violates the rules and regulations that are defined by the government of the country where it is being released. This may be unintentional but will impact negatively on the business.

Usually, the developed Product/application that is intended to be released all over the world, has to undergo RAT, as different countries/regions have different rules and regulations defined by its governing bodies.

If any of the rules and regulations are violated for any country, then that country or the specific region in that country will not be allowed to use the Product and is considered as a Failure. Vendors of the Product will be directly responsible if the Product is released even though there is a violation.

Operational Acceptance Testing (OAT)

This is to assess the operational readiness of the Product and is a non-functional testing. It mainly includes testing of recovery, compatibility, maintainability, technical support availability, reliability, fail-over, localization etc.

OAT mainly assures the stability of the Product before releasing it to the production.

Alpha Testing

This is to assess the Product in the development/testing environment by a specialized testers team usually called alpha testers. Here, the testers feedback, suggestions help to improve the Product usage and also to fix certain bugs.

Here, testing happens in a controlled manner.

Beta Testing/Field Testing

This is to assess the Product by exposing it to the real end-users, usually called beta testers/beta users, in their environment. Continuous feedback from the users is collected and the issues are fixed. Also, this helps in enhancing/improving the Product to give a rich user experience.

Testing happens in an uncontrolled manner, which means a user has no restrictions on the way in which the Product is being used.

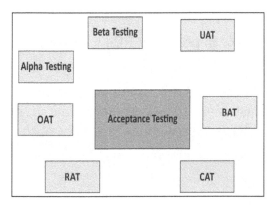

All these types have a common goal:

- Ensure to gain/enrich Confidence in the Product.

- Ensure that the Product is ready to be used by the real users.

Who does Acceptance Testing?

For Alpha type, only the members of the organization (who developed the Product) perform the testing. These members are not directly a part of the project (Project managers/leads, developers, testers). Management, Sales, Support teams usually perform the testing and provide feedback accordingly.

Apart from the Alpha type, all other acceptance types are generally performed by different stakeholders. Like customers, customer's customers, specialized testers from the organization (not always).

It is also good to involve Business Analysts and Subject Matter Expertise while performing this testing based on its type.

Qualities of Acceptance Testers

Testers with the below qualities are qualified as Acceptance testers:

- Ability to think logically and analytically.

- Good domain knowledge.

- Able to study the competitive products in the market and analyze the same in the developed product.

- Having end-user perception while testing.

- Understand business need for each requirement and test accordingly.

Impact of Issues Found During this Testing

Any issues encountered in Acceptance test phase should be considered as a high priority one and fixed immediately. This also requires Root Cause Analysis to be performed on each and every issue that is found.

The testing team plays a major role in providing RCA's for Acceptance issues. These also help in determining how efficiently testing is performed.

Also, valid issues in acceptance test will hit both the testing and the development team efforts in terms of impression, ratings, customer surveys, etc. Sometimes, if any ignorance from the testing team on validations is found, it leads to escalations as well.

Use

This testing is useful from several aspects. Few of which include:

- To figure out the issues missed during the functional testing phase.

- How well the Product is developed.

- A product is what actually the customers need.

- Feedbacks/surveys conducted help in improving the Product performance and user experience.

- Improve the process followed by having RCAs as input.

- Minimize or eliminate the issues arising from the Production Product.

Differences between System Testing, Acceptance Testing and User Acceptance Testing

Given below are the prime differences between these 3 types of Acceptance tests:

System Testing	Acceptance Testing	User Acceptance Testing
End-to-end testing is performed to verify whether Product meets all the specified requirements	Testing is performed to verify whether Product meets customer requirements for acceptability	Testing is performed to verify whether end-users requirements are fulfilled for acceptability
A product is tested as the whole focusing only on functional and non-functional needs	Product is tested for business needs – user acceptability, business goals, rules and regulations, operations, etc.	Product is tested only for user acceptability
Testing team performs System Testing	Customer, Customers' customers, tester (rarely), management, Sales, Support teams performs acceptance testing depending on the type of test carried out	Customer, Customers' customer, testers (rarely) performs user acceptance testing

Test cases are written and executed	Acceptance tests are written and executed	User Acceptance tests are written and executed
Can be functional and non-functional	Usually Functional, but non-functional in case of RAT, OAT, etc	Only Functional
Only test data is used for testing	Real-time data/production data is used for testing	Real-time data / Production data is used for testing
Positive and negative tests are performed	Usually Positive tests are performed	Only Positive tests are performed
Issues found are considered as bugs and fixed based on severity and priority	Issues found marks Product as Failure, and considered to be fixed immediately	Issues found marks Product as Failure and considered to be fixed immediately
Controlled manner of testing	Can be controlled or uncontrolled based on type of testing	Uncontrolled manner of testing
Testing on Development environment	Testing on Development environment or pre-production environment or production environment, based on type	Testing is always on Pre-Production environment
No assumptions, but if any can be communicated	No assumptions	No assumptions

Acceptance Tests

Similar to Product test cases, we do have acceptance tests. Acceptance tests are derived from User stories' acceptance criteria. These are usually the scenarios that are written at the high-level detailing on what the Product has to do under different conditions.

It does not give a clear picture on how to perform tests, as in test cases. Acceptance tests are written by Testers who have a complete grip on the Product, usually Subject Matter Expertise. All the tests written are reviewed by a customer and/or business analysts.

These tests executed during acceptance test. Along with acceptance tests, a detailed document on any set-ups to be done has to be prepared. It should include every minute detail with proper screenshots, set-up values, conditions, etc.

Acceptance Test Bed

Test Bed for this testing is similar to a regular test bed but is a separate one. Platform with all the required hardware, software, operating products, network set-up & configurations, server set-up & configurations, database set-up & configurations, licenses, plug-ins, etc., have to be set up very much alike the Production environment.

Acceptance test bed is a platform/environment where the designed acceptance tests will be executed. Before handing over the Acceptance test environment to the customer, it is a good practice to check for any environmental issues and stability of the Product.

If there is no separate environment set up for acceptance testing, a regular testing environment can be used for that purpose. But here, it will be messy as the test data from regular

System Testing, and the real-time data from acceptance testing are maintained in a single environment.

Acceptance test bed is usually set up on the customer-side (i.e., in the laboratory) and will have restricted access to the development and testing teams.

Teams will be required to access this environment through VMs/or specifically designed URLs using special access credentials, and all the access to this will be tracked. Nothing on this environment has to be added/modified/deleted without the customer's permission, and they should be notified of the changes that are made.

Entry and Exit Criteria for AT

Just as any other phase in the STLC, Acceptance testing does have a set of entry and exit criteria which are to be well-defined in Acceptance Test Plan.

This is the phase which starts right after System testing and ends before the Production launch. So, the Exit criteria of System testing becomes a part of the Entry criteria for AT. Similarly, the Exit criteria of AT become a part of Entry criteria for the Production Launch.

Entry Criteria

Given below are the conditions to be fulfilled before starting:

- Business requirements should be clear and available.
- System and Regression testing phase should be completed.
- All the Critical, Major & Normal bugs should be fixed and closed (Minor bugs accepted mainly are cosmetic bugs that do not disturb the usage of the product).
- Known issues list should be prepared and shared with the stakeholders.
- Acceptance Test Bed should be set up and high-level check should be performed for no environmental issues.
- System Testing phase should be signed-off letting the product to move to the AT phase (Usually done through Email communication).

Exit Criteria

There are certain conditions to be fulfilled by AT to let the product go for a Production Launch. They are as follows:

- Acceptance tests should be executed and all the tests should Pass.
- No Critical/Major defects left Open. All the defects should be fixed and verified immediately.
- AT should be Signed-off-by all the included stakeholders with Go/No-Go Decision on the product.

Acceptance Testing Process

In V-Model, AT phase is in parallel to the Requirements phase.

Actual AT process goes as shown below:

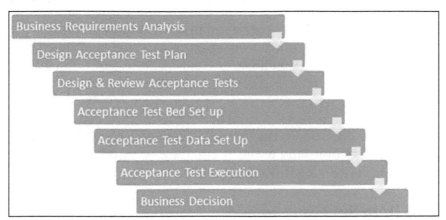

Business Requirements Analysis

Business requirements are analyzed by referring all the available documents within the project. Some of which are:

- System Requirement Specifications.

- Business Requirements Document.

- Use Cases.

- Workflow diagrams.

- Designed data matrix.

Design Acceptance Test Plan

There are certain items to be documented in the Acceptance Test Plan. Let's take a look at some of them:

- Acceptance Testing strategy and approach.

- Entry and exit criteria should be well-defined.

- The scope of AT should be well-mentioned and it has to cover only the business requirements.

- Acceptance test design approach should be detailed so as anyone writing tests can easily understand the way in which it has to be written.

- Test Bed set up, actual testing schedule/timelines should be mentioned.

- As testing is conducted by different stakeholders, details on logging bug should be mentioned as the stakeholders may not be aware of the procedure followed.

Design and Review Acceptance Tests

Acceptance tests should be written at a scenario level mentioning what has to be done (not in-detail to include how to do). These should be written only for the identified areas of scope for business requirements, and each and every test has to be mapped to its referencing requirement.

All the written acceptance tests have to be reviewed to achieve high coverage on business requirements. This is to make sure that any other tests apart from scope mentioned are not involved so that testing lies within the scheduled timelines.

Acceptance Test Bed Set up

Test Bed should be set up similar to a Production environment. Very high-level checks are required to confirm on environment stability and usage. Share the credentials to use the environment only with a stakeholder who is performing this testing.

Acceptance Test Data Set Up

Production data has to be prepared/populated as test data in the systems. Also, there should be a detailed document in such a way that the data has to be used for testing.

Do not have the test data like TestName1, TestCity1, etc., Instead have Albert, Mexico, etc. This gives a rich experience of real-time data and testing will be up-to-the-point.

Acceptance Test Execution

Designed Acceptance tests have to be executed on the environment at this step. Ideally, all the tests should pass at the first attempt itself. There should be no functional bugs arising out of Acceptance testing, if any then they should be reported at a high priority to be fixed.

Again, bugs fixed have to be verified and closed as a high priority task. Test execution report has to be shared on a daily basis.

Bugs logged in this phase should be discussed in a bug-triage meeting and has to undergo Root Cause Analysis procedure. This is the only point where acceptance testing assess whether all the business requirements are actually met by the product or not.

Business Decision

There comes out a Go/No-Go decision for the product to be launched in Production. Go decision will take the product ahead to be released to the market. No-Go decision marks the product as Failure.

Few factors of No-Go Decision:

- Poor Quality of the product.
- Too Many open Functional Bugs.
- Deviation from business requirements.

- Not up to the market standards and needs enhancements to match the current market standards.

Success Factors for this Testing

Once this test is planned, prepare a checklist which increases the success rate of it. There are some action items that are to be followed before Acceptance test starts.

They are:

- Have a well-defined scope and make sure there is a business need for the scope identified for this testing.

- Execute Acceptance tests in System testing phase itself at least once.

- Perform extensive ad-hoc testing for each of the acceptance test scenarios.

References

- Jerry Gao; H.-S. J. Tsao; Ye Wu (2003). Testing and Quality Assurance for Component-based Software. Artech House. pp. 170–. ISBN 978-1-58053-735-3

- Software-testing-introduction-importance: guru99.com, Retrieved 11 April, 2019

- Boehm, Barry W.; Papaccio, Philip N. (October 1988). "Understanding and Controlling Software Costs" (PDF). IEEE Transactions on Software Engineering. 14 (10): 1462–1477. doi:10.1109/32.6191. Retrieved 13 May, 2016

- Operational-acceptance-testing-oat: geeksforgeeks.org, Retrieved 07 June, 2019

- Jake Rogers (8 August 2016). "Common Questions Regarding Grey-Box Testing". cgsec.co.uk. Retrieved 8 August, 2016

- What-isinstallation-testing: softwaretestingclass.com, Retrieved 16 March, 2019

- Itkonen, J.; Rautiainen, K. (2005-11-01). Exploratory testing: a multiple case study. 2005 International Symposium on Empirical Software Engineering, 2005. pp. 10 pp.–. doi:10.1109/ISESE.2005.1541817. ISBN 978-0-7803-9507-7

- What-is-acceptance-testing: softwaretestinghelp.com, Retrieved 25 August, 2019

Applications of Software Engineering

Software engineering finds application in a variety of different fields. A few of these are systems development, computer aided design, computer graphics and web engineering. The diverse applications of software engineering in these fields have been thoroughly discussed in this chapter.

Software engineering applications are new idea, device or process. Innovations are the application of better solutions that meet new requirements, inarticulate needs or existing market needs. It is proficient through more effective products, processes, services, technologies, or new ideas that are readily available to markets, governments and society. Innovations are something original and novel, as a significant, new that "breaks into" the market or society. The exhaustive and widespread use of computers and the improvements in database technology have provided large data. The emerging growth of data in databases has generated an urgent need for efficient data mining techniques to discover useful informational knowledge.

SYSTEMS DEVELOPMENT

Software Engineering Concepts used in the field of Systems Development for defining, designing, testing, and implementing a new software application or program. It comprises of the internal development of customized systems, the establishment of database systems, or the attainment of third party developed software. In this system, written standards and techniques must monitor all information systems processing functions. The management of company must describe and execute standards and embrace suitable system development life cycle practice that manage the process of developing, acquiring, implementing, and maintaining computerized information systems and associated technology.

System development methodologies are promoted in order to improve the management and control of the software development process, structuring and simplifying the procedure, and standardizing the development process and product by stipulating actions to be done and methods to be used. It is often implicitly presumed that the use of a system development methodology will increase system development output and excellence.

System Development Management Life-cycle

It is maintained in management studies that effectual way to protect information and information systems is to incorporate security into every step of the system development process, from the initiation of a project to develop a system to its disposition. The manifold process that begins with the initiation, analysis, design, and implementation, and continues through the maintenance and disposal of the system, is called the System Development Life Cycle (SDLC). Walsham stated that system development life cycle is an approach to developing an information system or software product that is characterized by a linear sequence of steps that progress from start to finish without revisiting any previous step. It is one of the oldest systems development models and is commonly used. According to Dennis, Wixom, and Tegarden the systems development life cycle is the process of understanding how an information system (IS) can support business needs by designing a system, building it, and delivering it to user.

The SDLC model is basically a project management device that is used to plan, execute, and control systems development projects. System development life cycles are usually deliberated in terms of the conventional development using the waterfall model or the prototyping development spiral model. Major objectives of systems development lifecycle are to ensure that high quality systems are delivered, provide strong management controls over the projects, and maximize the productivity of the systems staff. In order to fulfil these objectives, the systems development lifecycle has many specific requirements that include being able to support projects and systems of various scopes and types, supporting all of the technical activities, supporting all of the management activities, being highly usable, and providing guidance on how to install it.

Phases of System Development

A system development project comprises of numerous phases, such as feasibility analysis, requirements analysis, software design, software coding, testing and debugging, installation and maintenance:

1. A feasibility study is employed to decide whether a project should proceed. This will include an initial project plan and budget estimates for future stages of the project. In the example of the development of a central ordering system, a feasibility study would look at how a new central ordering system might be received by the various departments and how costly the new system would be relative to improving each of these individual systems.

2. Requirement analysis recognizes the requirements for the system. This includes a detailed analysis of the specific problem being addressed or the expectations of a particular system. It can be said that analysis will coherent what the system is supposed to do. For the central ordering system, the analysis would cautiously scrutinize existing ordering systems and how to use the best aspects of those systems, while taking advantage of the potential benefits of more centralized systems.

3. The design phase consist of determining what programs are required and how they are going to interact, how each individual program is going to work, what the software interface is going to look like and what data will be required. System design may use tools such as flowcharts and pseudo-code to develop the specific logic of the system. For this central ordering system, the design phase would lay out the comprehensive steps of how orders would take place and who in the organization would be involved at each step.

4. Implementation stage includes the design which is to be translated into code. This requires choosing the most suitable programming language and writing the actual code needed to make the design work. In this stage, the central ordering system is essentially coded using a particular programming language. This would also include developing a user interface that the various departments are able to use efficiently.

5. Testing and debugging stage encompasses testing individual modules of the system as well as the system as a whole. This includes making sure the system actually does what is expected and that it runs on intended platforms. Testing during the early stages of a project may involve using a prototype, which meets some of the very basic requirements of the system but lacks many of the details. Testing of the central ordering system could take place in one department or use only a few key individuals. That makes it possible to recognize needed improvements before execution in all departments.

6. In Installation phase, the system is implemented so that it becomes part of the workflows of the organization. Some training may be needed to make sure employees get happy with using the system. At this stage, the central ordering system is installed in all departments, replacing the older system.

7. All systems need some types of maintenance. This may consist of minor updates to the system or more drastic changes due to unexpected circumstances. As the organization and its departments evolve, the ordering process may require some modifications. This makes it possible to get the most out of a new centralized system.

Phases of the System Development Cycle

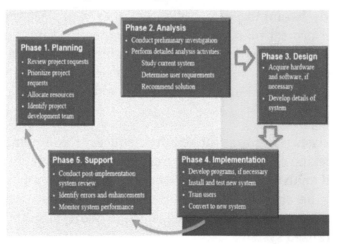

Whitten and Bentley recommended following categories of system development project lifecycle:

1. Planning

2. Analysis

3. Design

4. Implementation

5. Support

There are many different SDLC models and methodologies, but each usually consists of a series of defined steps such as Fountain, Spiral, rapid prototyping, for any SDLC model that is used, information security must be integrated into the SDLC to ensure appropriate protection for the information that the system will transmit, process, and store.

System Development Life-cycle Models

Fountain Model	Recognizes that there is considerable overlap of activities throughout the development cycle.
Spiral model	Emphasis the need to go back and reiterate earlier stages like a series of short water fall cycle, each producing an early prototype representing the part of entire cycle.
Build and fix model	Write some programming code, keeps modifying it until the customer is happy. Without planning this is very open ended and risky.
Rapid prototyping model	Emphasis is on creating a prototype that look and act like the desired product in order to test its usefulness. Once the prototype is approved, it is discarded and real software is written.
Incremental model	Divides the product into builds, where sections of the projects are created and tested separately.
Synchronize and stabilise model	Combines the advantages of spiral models with technology of overseeing and managing source code. This method allows many teams to work efficiently in parallel. It was defined by David Yoffe of Harvard University and Michael Cushman of Massachusetts institute of technology who studied Microsoft corporation developed internet explorer and how the Netscape communication corporation developed communicator finding common thread In the ways the two companies worked.

Waterfall Model

The Waterfall Model signifies a traditional type of system development project lifecycle. It builds upon the basic steps associated with system development project lifecycle and uses a top-down development cycle in completing the system.

Walsham outlined the steps in the Waterfall Model which are as under:

1. A preliminary evaluation of the existing system is conducted and deficiencies are then identified. This can be done by interviewing users of the system and consulting with support personnel.

2. The new system requirements are defined: In particular, the deficiencies in the existing system must be addressed with specific proposals for improvement.

3. The proposed system is designed: Plans are developed and delineated concerning the physical construction, hardware, operating systems, programming, communications, and security issues.

4. The new system is developed and the new components and programs are obtained and installed.

5. Users of the system are then trained in its use, and all aspects of performance are tested. If necessary, adjustments must be made at this stage.

6. The system is put into use: This can be done in various ways. The new system can be phased in, according to application or location, and the old system is gradually replaced. In some cases, it may be more cost-effective to shut down the old system and implement the new system all at once.

7. Once the new system is up and running for a while, it should be exhaustively evaluated. Maintenance must be kept up rigorously at all times.

8. Users of the system should be kept up-to-date concerning the latest modifications and procedures. On the basis of the Waterfall Model, if system developers find problems associated with a step, an effort is made to go back to the previous step or the specific step in which the problem occurred, and fix the problem by completing the step once more.

The Model's Development Schedule

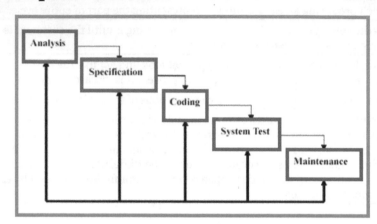

- Fountain model: The Fountain model is a logical enhancement to the Waterfall model. This model allows for the advancement from various stages of software development regardless of whether or not enough tasks have been completed to reach it.

- Prototyping Model: The prototyping paradigm starts with collecting the requirements. Developer and customer meet and define the overall objectives for the software, identify whatever requirements are known, and outline areas where further definition is mandatory. The prototype is appraised by the customer/user and used to improve requirements for the software to be developed. Iteration occurs as the prototype is tuned to satisfy the needs of the customer, while at the same time enabling the developer to better understand what needs to be done.

Major Advantages of this Model include:

- When prototype is presented to the user, he gets a proper clearness and functionality of the software and he can suggest changes and modifications.

- It determines the concept to prospective investors to get funding for project and thus gives clear view of how the software will respond.

- It decreases risk of failure, as potential risks can be recognized early and alleviation steps can be taken thus effective elimination of the potential causes is possible.

- Iteration between development team and client provides a very good and conductive environment during project. Both the developer side and customer side are coordinated.

- Time required to complete the project after getting final the SRS reduces, since the developer has a better idea about how he should approach the project.

Main drawbacks of this model are that Prototyping is typically done at the cost of the developer. So it should be done using nominal resources. It can be done using Rapid Application Development tools. Sometimes the start-up cost of building the development team, focused on making the prototype is high. Once developers get proper requirements from client after showing prototype model, it may be useless. It is a slow process and too much involvement of client is not always favoured by the creator.

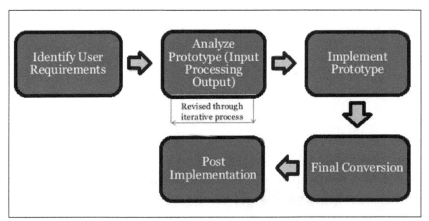

Different Phases of Prototyping Model.

Uses of prototyping:

- Verifying user needs
- Verifying that design = specifications
- Selecting the "best" design
- Developing a conceptual understanding of novel situations
- Testing a design under varying environments
- Demonstrating a new product to upper management
- Implementing a new system in the user environment quickly.

Rapid Application Development

This model is based on prototyping and iterative development with no detailed planning involved. The process of writing the software itself involves the planning required for developing the product. Rapid Application development focuses on gathering customer requirements through workshops or focus groups, early testing of the prototypes by the customer using iterative concept, reuse of the existing prototypes (components), continuous integration and rapid delivery.

There are three main phases to Rapid Application Development:

- Requirements planning
- RAD design workshop
- Implementation.

RAD Model

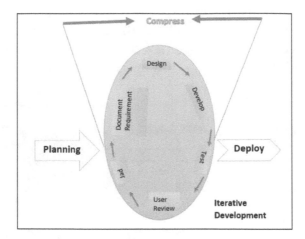

RAD is used when the team includes programmers and analysts who are experienced with it, there are pressing reasons for speeding up application development, the project involves a novel ecommerce application and needs quick results and users are sophisticated and highly engaged with the goals of the company.

Spiral Model

The spiral model was developed by Barry Boehm in 1988 (Boehm, 1986). This model is developed to Spiral Model to address the inadequacies of the Waterfall Model. Boehm stated that "the major distinguishing feature of the Spiral Model is that it creates a risk-driven approach to the software process rather than a primarily document-driven or code-driven process. It incorporates many of the strengths of other models and resolves many of their difficulties". A Spiral Model the first model to elucidate why the iteration matters. Spiral model is an evolutionary software process model which is a grouping of an iterative nature of prototyping and controlled and systematic aspects of traditional waterfall model. As originally proposed, the iterations were usually 6 months to 2 years long. Each phase starts with a design goal and ends with the client reviewing the progress. Analysis and engineering efforts are done at each phase of the project.

The spiral model consists of four phases:

- Planning

- Risk Analysis

- Engineering

- Evaluation

Major benefits of this model include:

- Changing requirements can be accommodated.

- Allows for extensive use of prototypes.

- Requirements can be captured more accurately.

- Users see the system early.

- Development can be divided in to smaller parts and more risky parts can be developed earlier which helps better risk management.

Main drawbacks of this model are as under:

1. Management is more complex

2. Conclusion of project may not be recognized early

3. Not suitable for small or low risk projects (expensive for small projects)

4. Process is difficult

5. Spiral may go indeterminately

6. Large numbers of intermediate stages require unnecessary documentation.

The spiral model is normally used in huge projects. For example, the military had adopted the spiral model for its Future Combat Systems program. The spiral model may suit small software applications.

Phases of Spiral Model

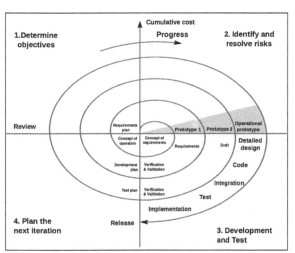

Incremental Model

Incremental model is a technique of software development in which the model is analysed, designed, tested, and implemented incrementally. Some benefits of this model are that it handles large projects, it has the functionality of the water fall and the prototyping model. It is easier to manage the project as it is broken down into smaller pieces, changes can be done through the development stages and errors are easy to be identified.

Disadvantages of this model are that when remedying a problem in a functional unit, then all the functional units will have to be corrected thus taking a lot of time. It needs good planning and designing.

Increment Model of SDLC

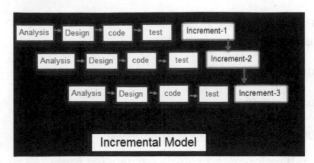

There are numerous benefits of integrating security into the system development life cycle that are as under:

1. Early documentation and alleviation of security vulnerabilities and problems with the configuration of systems, resulting in lower costs to implement security controls and mitigation of vulnerabilities.

2. Awareness of potential engineering challenges caused by mandatory security controls.

3. Identification of shared security services and reuse of security strategies and tools that will reduce development costs and improve the system's security posture through the application of proven methods and techniques.

4. Assistance of informed executive decision making through the application of a comprehensive risk management process in a timely manner.

5. Documentation of important security decisions made during the development process to inform management about security considerations during all phases of development.

6. Enhanced organization and customer confidence to facilitate adoption and use of systems, and improved confidence in the continued investment in government systems.

7. Improved systems interoperability and integration that would be difficult to achieve if security is considered separately at various system levels.

Strengths of System Development Life Cycle

1. Methodologies incorporating this approach have been well tried and tested.

2. This cycle divides development into distinct phases.

3. Makes tasks more manageable.

4. It Offers opportunity for more control over development process.

5. It Provides standards for documentation.

6. It is better than trial and error.

Weaknesses of System Development Life Cycle

1. It fails to realise the "big picture" of strategic management.

2. It is too inflexible to cope with changing requirements.

3. It stresses on "hard" thinking (which is often reflected in documentation that is too technical).

4. It unable to capture true needs of users.

Embedded System Development

An embedded system is a computer system with a dedicated function within a larger mechanical or electrical system that serves a more general purpose, often with real-time computing constraints. It is embedded as part of a complete device often including hardware and mechanical parts.

Embedded systems are designed to do some specific task, rather than be a general-purpose computer for multiple tasks. Some also have real-time performance constraints that must be met, for reasons such as safety and usability; others may have low or no performance requirements, allowing the system hardware to be simplified to reduce costs. Since the embedded system is dedicated to specific tasks, design engineers can optimize it to reduce the size and cost of the product and increase the reliability and performance. The processors used in embedded systems may be types ranging from rather general purpose to very specialized in certain class of computations, or even custom designed for the application at hand. A common standard class of dedicated processors is the digital signal processor (DSP).

The program instructions written for embedded systems are referred to as firmware, and are stored mainly in read-only memory or Flash memory chips. They run with limited computer hardware resources: little memory, small or non-existent keyboard or screen. As with other software, embedded system designers use compilers, assemblers, and debuggers to develop embedded system software. The embedded system interacts directly with hardware devices and mostly must respond, in real time, to events from the system's environment. In the real-time systems the embedded real-time software must react to events generated by the hardware and issue control signals in response to these events.

Embedded systems control many devices in common use today. They are commonly found in consumer, cooking, industrial, automotive, medical, commercial and military applications. Physically, embedded systems range from portable devices such as digital watches and MP3 players, to large stationary installations like traffic lights, factory controllers and largely complex systems like hybrid vehicles, MRI. Telecommunications systems employ numerous embedded systems from telephone to cell phones. Many household appliances, such as microwave ovens, washing machines and dishwashers, include embedded systems to provide flexibility, efficiency and features. Transportation systems from flight to automobiles increasingly use embedded systems.

Computers are used to control a wide range of systems from simple domestic machines to entire manufacturing plants. These computers interact directly with hardware devices. The software in these systems is embedded real-time software that must react to events generated by the hardware from the environment of system and issue control signals in response to these events.

Software failures are relatively usual. In most cases, these failures cause inconvenience but no serious, long-term damage. However, in some systems failure can result in significant economic losses, physical damage or threats to human life. These systems are called critical systems. Critical systems are technical or socio-technical systems that people or businesses depend on. If these systems fail to deliver their services as expected then serious problems and significant losses may result. Modern electronic systems increasingly make use of embedded computer systems to add functionality, increase flexibility, controllability and performance. However, the increased use of embedded software to control systems brings with it certain risks. This is especially significant in safety critical systems where human safety is dependent upon the correct operation of the system.

Critical Systems

There are three main types of critical systems:

1. Safety-critical systems: A system whose failure may result in injury, loss of life or serious environmental damage.

2. Mission-critical systems: A system whose failure may result in the failure of some goal-directed activity.

3. Business-critical systems: A system whose failure may result in very high costs for the business using that system.

The most important property of a critical system is its dependability. The term dependability covers the related systems attributes such as availability, reliability, safety and security.

There are three system components where critical systems failures may occur:

1. System hardware components may fail because of mistakes in their design or manufacturing errors.

2. System software may fail due to mistakes in its specification, design or implementation.

3. Human operators of the system may fail to operate the system correctly.

Because of the high cost of critical systems failure, trusted methods and well-known techniques must be used for development of these systems. Most critical systems are socio-technical systems where people monitor and control the operation of computer-based systems. Operators in these systems must successfully treat unexpected situations and cope with additional workload. However, this may cause more stress and so on mistakes.

System Dependability

The dependability is a property of systems. A dependable computer system provides a trustworthy operation to users. This means that system is expected to not fail in normal use. There are four principle attributes to dependability:

1. Availability: The availability of a system is the probability that the system can provide the services requested by users at any time.

2. Reliability: The reliability of a system is the probability, over a given period of time, that the system will correctly deliver services.

3. Safety: The safety of a system shows the extent of damage may be caused by the system to people or its environment.

4. Security: The security of a system shows that how the system can resist accidental or deliberate unauthorized intrusions.

Besides these four attributes, other system properties can also be related to dependability:

1. Reparability: Disruption caused by any failure can be minimized if the system can be repaired as soon as possible. Therefore, it is important to be able to diagnose the problem, access the component that has failed and make changes to fix that component.

2. Maintainability: Once new requirements are emerged it is important to maintain the system by integration of new functionalities required.

3. Survivability: Survivability is the ability of a system to continue operation of the service during a possible attack, even at the loss of certain parts of the system.

4. Error tolerance: This property is considered as part of usability and shows how the system is designed to avoid and tolerate user input errors.

System developers have usually to prioritize system performance and system dependability. Generally, high levels of dependability can only be achieved at the expense of system performance. Because of the additional design, implementation and validation costs, increasing the dependability of a system can significantly increase development costs.

Availability and Reliability

The reliability of a system is the probability that the system correctly provides services as defined in its specification. In other words, the reliability of software can be related to the probability that the system input will be a member of the set of inputs, which cause an erroneous output to occur. If an input causing an erroneous output is associated with a frequently used part of the program, then failures will be frequent. However, if it is associated with rarely used code, then users will hardly complain about failures.

The availability of a system is the probability that the system will provide its services to users when they request them. If users need for continuous service then the availability requirements are high. Reliability and availability are primarily compromised by system failures. These may be a failure to provide a service, a failure to deliver a service as specified, or the delivery of a service unsafely and insecurely. However, many failures are a consequence of erroneous system behaviour that derives from faults in the system. To increase the reliability of a system the following approaches can be used:

1. Fault avoidance: Program development techniques are used that can minimize the possibility of mistakes and/or eliminate mistakes before they cause system faults.

2. Fault detection and removal: The use of verification and validation techniques that effectively helps to detect and remove the faults before the system is used.

3. Fault tolerance: Techniques that ensure that faults in a system do not result in system errors or that ensure that system errors do not result in system failures.

Safety

The essential feature of safety-critical systems is that system operation is always safe. These systems never compromise or damage people or the environment of the system, even if the system fail. Safety-critical software has two groups:

1. Primary safety-critical software: This software is usually embedded as a controller in a system. Malfunctioning of such software can cause a hardware malfunction, which results in human injury and/or environmental damage.

2. Secondary safety-critical software: This is software that can indirectly result in injury. For an example, software used for design has a fault can causes the malfunction of designed system and this may results in injury to people.

The safe operation, i.e. ensuring either that accidents do not occur or that the consequences of an accident are minimal, can be achieved in the next ways:

1. Hazard avoidance: This type of system is designed so that hazards are avoided. For example, a safe cutting system equipped with two control buttons, where the two buttons can be operated by using separate hands.

2. Hazard detection and removal: The system is designed so that hazards are detected and removed before they result in an accident. For example, pressure control in a chemical reactor system can reduce the detected excessive pressure before an explosion occurs.

3. Damage limitation: These systems have a functionality that can minimize the effects of an accident. For example, automatic fire extinguisher systems.

Security

Security has become increasingly important attributes of systems connecting to the Internet. Internet connections provide additional system functionality, but it also allows systems to be attacked by people with hostile intentions. Security is a system attribute that shows the ability of the system to protect itself from against accidental or deliberate external attacks. In some critical systems such as systems for electronic commerce, military systems, etc., security is the most important attribute of system dependability.

Examples of attacks might be viruses, unauthorized use of system services and data, unauthorized modification of the system, etc. Security is an important attribute for all critical systems. Without a reasonable level of security, the availability, reliability and safety of the system may be compromised if external attacks cause some damage to the system.

There are three types of damage that may be caused by external attack:

1. Denial of service: In this case of attack the system is forced into a state where its normal services become unavailable.

2. Corruption of programs or data: The software components of the system are damaged affecting reliability and safety of system.

3. Disclosure of confidential information: Confidential information managed by the system is exposed to unauthorized people as a consequence of the external attack.

The security of a system may be assured using the following methods:

1. Vulnerability avoidance: The system is designed not to be vulnerable. For example, if a system is not connected to Internet there is no possibility of external attacks.

2. Attack detection and neutralization: The system is designed so that it detects and removes vulnerabilities before any damage occurs. An example of vulnerability detection and removal is the use of a virus checker to remove infected files.

3. Exposure limitation: In these methods the consequences of attack are minimized. An example of exposure limitation is the application of regular system backups.

Critical Systems Development

Due to the quick progress in computer technology, improvement of software development methods, better programming languages and effective quality management the dependability of software has significantly improved in the last two decades. In system development special development techniques may be used to ensure that the system is safe, secure and reliable. There are three complementary approaches can be used to develop dependable software:

1. Fault avoidance: The design and implementation process are used to minimize the programming errors and so on the number of faults in a program.

2. Fault detection: The verification and validation processes are designed to discover and remove faults in a program before it is deployed for operational use.

3. Fault tolerance: The system is designed so that faults or unexpected system behaviour during execution is detected and managed in such a way that system failure does not occur.

Redundancy and diversity are fundamental to the achievement of dependability in any system. Examples of redundancy are the components of critical systems that replicate the functionality of other components or an additional checking mechanism that is added to system but not strictly necessary for the basic operation of system. Faults can therefore be detected before they cause failures, and the system may be able to continue operating if individual components fail. If the redundant components are not the same as other components, is the case of diversity, a common failure in the same, replicated component will not result in a complete system failure.

Software engineering research intended to develop tools, techniques and methodologies that lead to the production of fault-free software. Fault-free software is software that exactly meets its specification. Of course, this does not mean that the software will never fail. There may be errors in the specification that may be reflected in the software, or the users may misunderstand or misuse the software system. In order to develop fault-free software the following software engineering techniques must be used:

1. Dependable software processes: The use of a dependable software process with appropriate verification and validation activities can minimize the number of faults in a program and detect those that do slip through.

2. Quality management: The software development organization must have a development culture in which quality drives the software process. Design and development standards should be established that provide the development of fault-free programs.

3. Formal specification: There must be a precise system specification that defines the system to be implemented.

4. Static verification: Static verification techniques, such as the use of static analysers, can find anomalous program features that could be faults.

5. Strong typing: A strongly typed programming language such as Java must be used for development. If the programming language has strong typing, the language compiler can detect many programming errors.

6. Safe programming: Some programming language constructs are more complex and error-prone than others. Safe programming means avoiding or at least minimizing the use of these constructs.

7. Protected information: Design and implementation processes based on information hiding and encapsulation is to be followed. Object-oriented languages such as Java satisfy this condition.

Although, development of fault-free software by application of these techniques is possible, it is economically disadvantageous. The cost of finding and removing remaining faults rises exponentially as faults in the program are discovered and removed. While the software becomes more dependable more tests are needed to find fewer and fewer faults.

Fault Tolerance

A fault-tolerant system can continue its operation even after some of its part is faulty or not reliable. The fault-tolerance mechanisms in the system ensure that these system faults do not cause system failure. Where system failure could cause a catastrophic accident or where a loss of system operation would cause large economic losses it is necessary to develop fault-tolerant system.

There are four complementary approaches to ensure fault-tolerance of a system:

1. Fault detection: The system must detect a fault that causes a system failure. Generally, this based on checking consistency of the system state.

2. Damage assessment: The parts of the system state that have been affected by the fault must be detected.

3. Fault recovery: The system restores its state to a known safe state. This may be achieved by correcting the damaged state or by restoring the system to a known safe state.

4. Fault repair: This involves modifying the system so that the fault does not recur.

Fault Detection and Damage Assessment

The first stage in ensuring fault tolerance is to detect that a fault either has occurred or will occur unless some action is taken immediately. To achieve this, the illegal values of state variables must be recognized. Therefore, it is necessary to define state constraints that define the conditions that must always hold for all legal states. If these predicates are false, then a fault has occurred.

Damage assessment involves analyzing the system state to estimate the extent of the state corruption. The role of the damage assessment procedures is not to recover from the fault but to assess what parts of the state space have been affected by the fault. Damage can only be assessed if it is possible to apply some validity function that checks whether the state is consistent.

Fault Recovery and Repair

The purpose of fault recovery process is to modify the state of the system so that the effects of the fault are eliminated or reduced. The system can continue to operate, perhaps in some degraded form. Forward recovery tries to correct the damaged system state and to create the intended state. Forward recovery is only possible in the cases where the state information includes built-in redundancy. Backward recovery restores the system state to a known correct state.

For an example, most database systems include backward error recovery. When a user starts a database operation, a transaction is initiated. The changes made during that transaction are not immediately incorporated in the database. The database is only updated after the transaction is finished and no problems are detected. If the transaction fails, the database is not updated.

Real-time Software Design

The real-time embedded systems are significantly different from other types of software systems. Their correct operation is dependent on the system responding to events within a short time interval. The real-time system can be shortly defined as follows:

A real-time system is a software system where the correct operation of the system depends on the results produced by the system and the time at which these results are produced. Timely response is an important factor in all embedded systems but, in some cases, very fast response is not necessary. The real-time system is a stimulus/response system. It must produce a corresponding response for a particular input stimulus. Therefore, the behaviour of a real-time system can therefore be defined by listing the stimuli received by the system, the associated responses and the time at which the response must be produced.

Stimuli has two classes:

1. Periodic stimuli: These stimuli are generated at predictable time intervals.

2. Aperiodic stimuli: These stimuli occur irregularly.

Periodic stimuli in a real-time system are usually generated by sensors associated with the system and provide information about the state of the system's environment. The responses of system are transmitted to actuators that may control some equipment. Aperiodic stimuli may be generated either by the actuators or by sensors. This sensor-system-actuator model of an embedded real-time system is illustrated in figure.

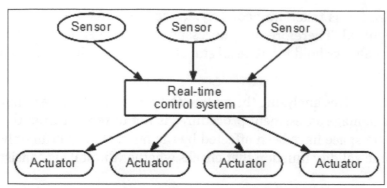

General model for a real-time system.

A real-time system must able to respond to stimuli that occur at different times. Therefore, architecture should be designed so that, as soon as a stimulus is received, control is transferred to the correct handler. This cannot be achieved using sequential programs. Consequently, real-time systems are normally designed as a set of concurrent and cooperating processes. In order to manage these concurrent processes most real-time systems includes a real-time operating system.

The stimulus-response model of a real-time system consists of three processes. Each type of sensor has a sensor management process, computational processes to compute the required response for the stimuli received by the system and control processes for actuator to manage their operation. This stimulus-response model enables rapid collection of data from the sensor and allows the computational processes and actuator responses to be carried out later.

System Design

Designing a real-time system it is necessary to decide first which system capabilities are to be implemented in software and which in hardware. Then the design process of real-time software focuses on the stimuli rather than the objects and functions. The design process has a number of overlapped stages:

1. Identification of the stimuli that the system must process and the associated responses.

2. Specifying the timing constraints for each stimulus and associated response.

3. Selection of hardware components and the real-time operating system to be used.

4. Aggregation of the stimulus and response processing into a number of concurrent processes. It is usual in real-time systems design is to associate a concurrent process with each class of stimulus and response as shown in figure.

5. Design of algorithms of the required computations for each stimulus and response.

6. Design a scheduling system ensuring that processes are started and completed in time.

Processes must be coordinated in a real-time system. Process coordination mechanisms ensure mutual exclusion to shared resources. Once the process architecture has been designed and scheduling policy has been decided it should be checked that the system will meet its timing requirements. Timing constraints or other requirements often mean that some system functions, such as signal processing, should be implemented in hardware rather than in software. Hardware components can provide a better performance than the equivalent software.

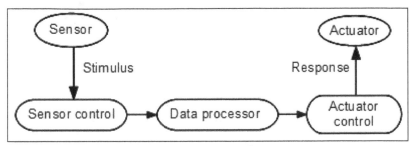

Sensor – actuator control process.

Real-time System Modelling

Real-time systems have to respond to events occurring at irregular intervals. These stimuli often cause the system to move to a new state. For this reason, state machine models are often used to model real-time systems. Application of state machine models is an effective way to represent the design of a real-time system. The UML supports the development of state models based on state-charts. A state model of a system assumes that the system, at any time, is in one of a number of possible states. When a stimulus is received it may cause a transition to a different state.

Real-time Operating Systems

Most of the embedded systems have real-time performance constraints that mean they have to work in conjunction with a real-time operating system (RTOS). Real-time operating systems guarantee a certain capability within a specified time constrain. It manages processes and resource allocation in a real-time system. It can starts and stops processes and allocate memory and processor resources, so that stimuli can be handled as concurrent processes.

Real-time operating systems usually include the following components:

1. Real-time clock: This provides information to schedule processes periodically.

2. Interrupt handler: This manages aperiodic requests for service.

3. Process manager: It is responsible for scheduling processes to be executed.

4. Resource manager: Resource manager allocates resources (memory, processor, etc.) to processes.

5. Despatcher: It is responsible for starting the execution of a process.

Process Management

Real-time systems have to respond events from the hardware in real time. The processes handling events must be scheduled for execution and must be allocated processor resources to provide their deadline. In real-time operating systems the process manager is responsible for selecting the next process to be executed, allocating resources such as processor and memory resources and starting and stopping the process.

The process manager has to manage processes having different priority. Real-time operating systems define different priority levels for system processes:

1. Interrupt level: This is the highest priority level. It is allocated to processes that need a very fast response.

2. Clock level: This level of priority is assigned to periodic processes.

3. Background processes level: This is the lowest priority level. It is allocated to background processes that have no timing constraints. These processes are scheduled for execution when processor capacity is available.

In most real-time systems, there are several types of periodic processes. They usually control the data acquisition and the actions of actuators. Periodic processes have different execution time and deadline. The timing requirements of all processes are specified by the application program. The real-time operating system manages the execution of periodic processes and ensures that every process have to be completed by their deadline.

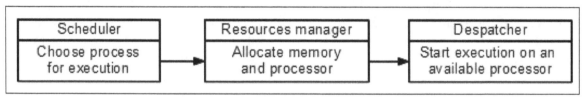

RTOS actions required to start a process.

Figure shows the sequence of activities that are performed by the operating system for periodic process management. The scheduler examines all the periodic processes and chooses a process to be executed. The choice depends on the process priority, the process periods, the expected execution times and the deadlines of the ready processes.

COMPUTER AIDED DESIGN

Computer-aided design (CAD) is the use of computers (or workstations) to aid in the creation, modification, analysis, or optimization of a design. CAD software is used to increase the productivity of the designer, improve the quality of design, improve communications through documentation, and to create a database for manufacturing. CAD output is often in the form of electronic files for print, machining, or other manufacturing operations. The term CADD (for *Computer Aided Design and Drafting*) is also used.

Its use in designing electronic systems is known as electronic design automation (EDA). In mechanical design it is known as mechanical design automation (MDA) or computer-aided drafting (CAD), which includes the process of creating a technical drawing with the use of computer software.

CAD software for mechanical design uses either vector-based graphics to depict the objects of traditional drafting, or may also produce raster graphics showing the overall appearance of designed objects. However, it involves more than just shapes. As in the manual drafting of technical and engineering drawings, the output of CAD must convey information, such as materials, processes, dimensions, and tolerances, according to application-specific conventions.

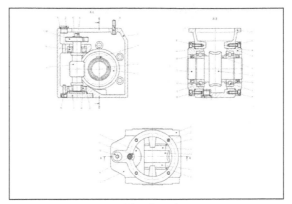

2D CAD drawing

CAD may be used to design curves and figures in two-dimensional (2D) space; or curves, surfaces, and solids in three-dimensional (3D) space.

CAD is an important industrial art extensively used in many applications, including automotive, shipbuilding, and aerospace industries, industrial and architectural design, prosthetics, and many more. CAD is also widely used to produce computer animation for special effects in movies, advertising and technical manuals, often called DCC digital content creation. The modern ubiquity and power of computers means that even perfume bottles and shampoo dispensers are designed using techniques unheard of by engineers of the 1960s. Because of its enormous economic importance, CAD has been a major driving force for research in computational geometry, computer graphics (both hardware and software), and discrete differential geometry.

The design of geometric models for object shapes, in particular, is occasionally called *computer-aided geometric design* (*CAGD*). Starting around the mid 1960s, with the IBM Drafting System, computer-aided design systems began to provide more capability than just an ability to reproduce manual drafting with electronic drafting, the cost-benefit for companies to switch to CAD became apparent. The benefits of CAD systems over manual drafting are the capabilities one often takes for granted from computer systems today; automated generation of bills of materials, auto layout in integrated circuits, interference checking, and many others. Eventually, CAD provided the designer with the ability to perform engineering calculations. During this transition, calculations were still performed either by hand or by those individuals who could run computer programs. CAD was a revolutionary change in the engineering industry, where draftsmen, designers and engineering roles begin to merge. It did not eliminate departments as much as it merged departments and empowered draftsman, designers, and engineers. CAD is an example of the pervasive effect computers were beginning to have on industry. Current computer-aided design software packages range from 2D vector-based drafting systems to 3D solid and surface modelers. Modern CAD packages can also frequently allow rotations in three dimensions, allowing viewing of a designed object from any desired angle, even from the inside looking out. Some CAD software is capable of dynamic mathematical modeling.

CAD technology is used in the design of tools and machinery and in the drafting and design of all types of buildings, from small residential types (houses) to the largest commercial and industrial structures (hospitals and factories).

3D CAD model

CAD is mainly used for detailed engineering of 3D models or 2D drawings of physical components, but it is also used throughout the engineering process from conceptual design and layout of products, through strength and dynamic analysis of assemblies to definition of manufacturing methods of components. It can also be used to design objects such as jewelry, furniture, appliances, etc. Furthermore, many CAD applications now offer advanced rendering and animation capabilities so engineers can better visualize their product designs. 4D BIM is a type of virtual construction engineering simulation incorporating time or schedule related information for project management.

CAD has become an especially important technology within the scope of computer-aided technologies, with benefits such as lower product development costs and a greatly shortened design cycle. CAD enables designers to layout and develops work on screen, print it out and save it for future editing, saving time on their drawings.

Uses

Computer-aided design is one of the many tools used by engineers and designers and is used in many ways depending on the profession of the user and the type of software in question. CAD is one part of the whole digital product development (DPD) activity within the product lifecycle management (PLM) processes, and as such is used together with other tools, which are either integrated modules or stand-alone products, such as:

- Computer-aided engineering (CAE) and finite element analysis (FEA).

- Computer-aided manufacturing (CAM) including instructions to computer numerical control (CNC) machines.

- Photorealistic rendering and motion simulation.

- Document management and revision control using product data management (PDM).

CAD is also used for the accurate creation of photo simulations that are often required in the preparation of environmental impact reports, in which computer-aided designs of intended buildings are superimposed into photographs of existing environments to represent what that locale will be like, where the proposed facilities are allowed to be built. Potential blockage of view corridors and shadow studies are also frequently analyzed through the use of CAD.

CAD has been proven to be useful to engineers as well. Using four properties which are history, features, parameterization, and high-level constraints. The construction history can be used to look back into the model's personal features and work on the single area rather than the whole model. Parameters and constraints can be used to determine the size, shape, and other properties of the different modeling elements. The features in the CAD system can be used for the variety of tools for measurement such as tensile strength, yield strength, electrical or electromagnetic properties. Also its stress, strain, timing or how the element gets affected in certain temperatures, etc.

Types

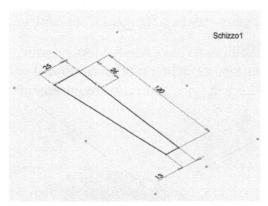

A simple procedure

There are several different types of CAD, each requiring the operator to think differently about how to use them and design their virtual components in a different manner for each.

There are many producers of the lower-end 2D systems, including a number of free and open-source programs. These provide an approach to the drawing process without all the fuss over scale and placement on the drawing sheet that accompanied hand drafting since these can be adjusted as required during the creation of the final draft.

3D wireframe is basically an extension of 2D drafting (not often used today). Each line has to be manually inserted into the drawing. The final product has no mass properties associated with it and cannot have features directly added to it, such as holes. The operator approaches these in a similar fashion to the 2D systems, although many 3D systems allow using the wireframe model to make the final engineering drawing views.

3D "dumb" solids are created in a way analogous to manipulations of real-world objects (not often used today). Basic three-dimensional geometric forms (prisms, cylinders, spheres, and so on) have solid volumes added or subtracted from them as if assembling or cutting real-world objects. Two-dimensional projected views can easily be generated from the models. Basic 3D solids don't usually include tools to easily allow motion of components, set limits to their motion, or identify interference between components.

There are two types of 3D solid modeling:

- *Parametric modeling* allows the operator to use what is referred to as "design intent". The objects and features created are modifiable. Any future modifications can be made by changing how the original part was created. If a feature was intended to be located from the center of the part, the operator should locate it from the center of the model. The feature could be located using any geometric object already available in the part, but this random placement would defeat the design intent. If the operator designs the part as it functions the parametric modeler is able to make changes to the part while maintaining geometric and functional relationships.

- *Direct or explicit modeling* provide the ability to edit geometry without a history tree. With direct modeling, once a sketch is used to create geometry the sketch is incorporated into the new geometry and the designer just modifies the geometry without needing the original sketch. As with parametric modeling, direct modeling has the ability to include relationships between selected geometry (e.g., tangency, concentricity).

Top end systems offer the capabilities to incorporate more organic, aesthetics and ergonomic features into designs. Freeform surface modeling is often combined with solids to allow the designer to create products that fit the human form and visual requirements as well as they interface with the machine.

Technology

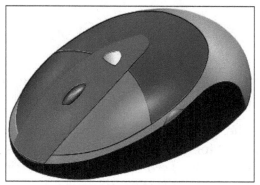

A CAD model of a computer mouse.

Originally software for CAD systems was developed with computer languages such as Fortran, ALGOL but with the advancement of object-oriented programming methods this has radically changed. Typical modern parametric feature-based modeler and freeform surface systems are built around a number of key C modules with their own APIs. A CAD system can be seen as built up from the interaction of a graphical user interface (GUI) with NURBS geometry or boundary representation (B-rep) data via a geometric modeling kernel. A geometry constraint engine may also be employed to manage the associative relationships between geometry, such as wireframe geometry in a sketch or components in an assembly.

Unexpected capabilities of these associative relationships have led to a new form of prototyping called digital prototyping. In contrast to physical prototypes, which entail manufacturing time in the design. That said, CAD models can be generated by a computer after the physical prototype has been scanned using an industrial CT scanning machine. Depending on the nature of the business, digital or physical prototypes can be initially chosen according to specific needs.

Today, CAD systems exist for all the major platforms (Windows, Linux, UNIX and Mac OS X); some packages support multiple platforms.

Currently, no special hardware is required for most CAD software. However, some CAD systems can do graphically and computationally intensive tasks, so a modern graphics card, high speed (and possibly multiple) CPUs and large amounts of RAM may be recommended.

The human-machine interface is generally via a computer mouse but can also be via a pen and digitizing graphics tablet. Manipulation of the view of the model on the screen is also sometimes done with the use of a Spacemouse/SpaceBall. Some systems also support stereoscopic glasses for viewing the 3D model. Technologies which in the past were limited to larger installations or specialist applications have become available to a wide group of users. These include the CAVE or HMDs and interactive devices like motion-sensing technology

Software

CAD software enables engineers and architects to design, inspect and manage engineering projects within an integrated graphical user interface (GUI) on a personal computer system. Most applications support solid modeling with boundary representation (B-Rep) and NURBS geometry, and enable the same to be published in a variety of formats. A geometric modeling kernel is a software component that provides solid modeling and surface modeling features to CAD applications.

Based on market statistics, commercial software from Autodesk, Dassault Systems, Siemens PLM Software, and PTC dominate the CAD industry. The following is a list of major CAD applications, grouped by usage statistics.

Commercial

- AgiliCity Modelur
- Autodesk AutoCAD
- Bricsys BricsCAD
- Dassault Systemes CATIA
- Dassault Systemes SolidWorks
- Kubotek KeyCreator
- PTC PTC Creo (formerly known as Pro/ENGINEER)
- Siemens Solid Edge
- Trimble SketchUp
- Alibre Design
- AllyCAD
- Autodesk Inventor
- AxSTREAM
- Bentley Systems - MicroStation
- Cobalt

- IRONCAD
- MEDUSA
- Onshape
- ProgeCAD
- Promine
- PunchCAD
- Remo 3D
- Rhinoceros 3D
- RoutCad
- Siemens NX
- SketchUp
- SpaceClaim
- T-FLEX CAD
- TurboCAD
- VariCAD.

Freeware and Open Source

- 123D
- BRL-CAD
- BricsCAD Shape
- FreeCAD
- LibreCAD
- QCad
- OpenSCAD
- SolveSpace.

CAD Kernels

- Parasolid by Siemens
- ACIS by Spatial
- ShapeManager by Autodesk
- Open CASCADE
- C3D by C3D Labs.

COMPUTER GRAPHICS

Pioneers in Computer Graphics

1. Charles Csuri: Charles Csuri is a pioneer in computer animation and digital fine art and created the first computer art in 1964. Csuri was recognized by *Smithsonian* as the father of digital art and computer animation, and as a pioneer of computer animation by the Museum of Modern Art (MoMA) and Association for Computing Machinery-SIGGRAPH.

2. Donald P. Greenberg: Donald P. Greenberg is a leading innovator in computer graphics. Greenberg has authored hundreds of articles and served as a teacher and mentor to many prominent computer graphic artists, animators, and researchers such as Robert L. Cook, Marc Levoy, Brian A. Barsky, and Wayne Lytle. Many of his former students have won Academy Awards for technical achievements and several have won the SIGGRAPH Achievement Award. Greenberg was the founding director of the NSF Center for Computer Graphics and Scientific Visualization.

3. A. Michael Noll: Noll was one of the first researchers to use a digital computer to create artistic patterns and to formalize the use of random processes in the creation of visual arts. He began creating digital art in 1962, making him one of the earliest digital artists. In 1965, Noll along with Frieder Nake and Georg Nees were the first to publicly exhibit their computer art. During April 1965, the Howard Wise Gallery exhibited Noll's computer art along with random-dot patterns by Bela Julesz.

Other Pioneers

A modern render of the Utah teapot, an iconic model in 3D computer graphics created by Martin Newell

- Pierre Bézier
- Jim Blinn
- Jack Bresenham
- John Carmack
- Paul de Casteljau
- Ed Catmull

- Frank Crow
- James D. Foley
- William Fetter
- Henry Fuchs
- Henri Gouraud
- Charles Loop
- Nadia Magnenat Thalmann
- Benoît B. Mandelbrot
- Martin Newell
- Fred Parke
- Bui Tuong Phong
- David Pearson
- Steve Russell
- Daniel J. Sandin
- Alvy Ray Smith
- Bob Sproull
- Ivan Sutherland
- Daniel Thalmann
- Andries van Dam
- John Warnock
- J. Turner Whitted
- Lance Williams
- Jim Kajiya.

Organizations

- SIGGRAPH
- SIGGRAPH Asia
- GDC
- Bell Telephone Laboratories
- United States Armed Forces, particularly the Whirlwind computer and SAGE Project
- Boeing

- IBM
- Renault
- The computer science department of the University of Utah
- Lucasfilm and Industrial Light & Magic
- Autodesk
- Adobe Systems
- Pixar
- Silicon Graphics, Khronos Group & OpenGL
- The DirectX division at Microsoft
- Nvidia
- AMD.

Study of Computer Graphics

The study of computer graphics is a sub-field of computer science which studies methods for digitally synthesizing and manipulating visual content. Although the term often refers to three-dimensional computer graphics, it also encompasses two-dimensional graphics and image processing.

As an academic discipline, computer graphics studies the manipulation of visual and geometric information using computational techniques. It focuses on the *mathematical* and *computational* foundations of image generation and processing rather than purely aesthetic issues. Computer graphics is often differentiated from the field of visualization, although the two fields have many similarities.

Applications

Computer graphics may be used in the following areas:

- Computational biology
- Computational photography
- Computational physics
- Computer-aided design
- Computer simulation
- Design
- Digital art
- Education
- Graphic design

- Infographics
- Information visualization
- Rational drug design
- Scientific visualization
- Special Effects for cinema
- Video Games
- Virtual reality
- Web design.

WEB ENGINEERING

The concept of software engineering was first introduced in 1968 at the NATO Science Engineering conference held in Garmisch, Germany, to discuss the ominous "software crisis ." The software crisis was a result of informal development practices used to meet the needs of a rapidly changing hardware industry. Software applications were often noted as being unreliable, complex, expensive and sometimes delivered years after the deadline.

Since the inception of software engineering, tremendous strides have been made to develop effective strategies to deliver reliable, cost-efficient software.

Yet, with the advent of the World Wide Web, the topic of how to deliver trustworthy, cost-efficient web applications has become one of increasing importance. Software applications no longer run on a local machine and are accessed by only those who are part of the organization. Now, users demand that software be accessible wherever they are which brings a whole new notion to the delivery of reliable, cost-efficient software. Consequently, the role of software engineering is changing to meet the demands of the heterogeneous user.

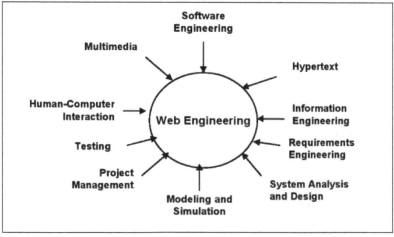

Web engineering

Web engineering is an emerging multi-disciplinary field that is concerned with the development of web-based applications and systems . As stated by Ginige and Murugesan, the premise of web engineering is a proactive approach taken to successfully manage the diversity and complexity of web application development and to avoid potential failures . Consequently, web engineering encompasses not only the technical aspects of software engineering and its traditional software processes, but also the business-related area of project management, and the humanistic side of computer science, human-computer interaction. Figure is a representation of the many disciplines that provide the foundation for web engineering.

Web Engineering Activities

Since web engineering deals with all aspects of web based system development, it too has many different activities akin to software engineering. These activities begin with specification, and continue with development, validation and evolution. However, specific web engineering activities include:

- Requirements engineering for web applications
- Techniques and methodologies for modeling web applications
- Design of functionality and interaction
- Implementation using a language for web-based applications
- Performance evaluation including verification and validation
- Operation and maintenance.

Even more specific to web engineering activities are those that focus on the interaction between the application and the user. Activities that focus on the humanistic side of web development include:

- Human and cultural aspects
- User involvement and feedback
- End-user application development
- Education and training
- Team and staff development.

References

- Farin, Gerald; Hoschek, Josef; Kim, Myung-Soo (2002). Handbook of computer aided geometric design [electronic resource]. Elsevier. ISBN 978-0-444-51104-1
- Systems-development, Management: civilserviceindia.com, Retrieved 09 June, 2019
- Mecha-tananyag, szoftverfejlesztesi-folyamatok-angol: autolab.unipannon.hu, Retrieved 21 August, 2019
- "3D Feature-based, Parametric Solid Modeling". engineershandbook.com. Archived from the original on 2012-11-18. Retrieved 2012-03-01

PERMISSIONS

We would like to thank the editorial team for lending their expertise to make the book truly unique. They have played a crucial role in the development of this book. Without their invaluable contributions this book wouldn't have been possible. They have made vital efforts to compile up to date information on the varied aspects of this subject to make this book a valuable addition to the collection of many professionals and students.

This book was conceptualized with the vision of imparting up-to-date and integrated information in this field. To ensure the same, a matchless editorial board was set up. Every individual on the board went through rigorous rounds of assessment to prove their worth. After which they invested a large part of their time researching and compiling the most relevant data for our readers.

The editorial board has been involved in producing this book since its inception. They have spent rigorous hours researching and exploring the diverse topics which have resulted in the successful publishing of this book. They have passed on their knowledge of decades through this book. To expedite this challenging task, the publisher supported the team at every step. A small team of assistant editors was also appointed to further simplify the editing procedure and attain best results for the readers.

Apart from the editorial board, the designing team has also invested a significant amount of their time in understanding the subject and creating the most relevant covers. They scrutinized every image to scout for the most suitable representation of the subject and create an appropriate cover for the book.

The publishing team has been an ardent support to the editorial, designing and production team. Their endless efforts to recruit the best for this project, has resulted in the accomplishment of this book. They are a veteran in the field of academics and their pool of knowledge is as vast as their experience in printing. Their expertise and guidance has proved useful at every step. Their uncompromising quality standards have made this book an exceptional effort. Their encouragement from time to time has been an inspiration for everyone.

The publisher and the editorial board hope that this book will prove to be a valuable piece of knowledge for students, practitioners and scholars across the globe.

INDEX